When
FOOTBALL *Was*
FOOTBALL

WEST BROMWICH ALBION

First published in 2013

A catalogue record for this book is available from the British Library

ISBN: 978-0-85733-194-6

Published by Haynes Publishing, Sparkford, Yeovil,
Somerset BA22 7JJ, UK
Tel: 01963 442030 Fax: 01963 440001
Int. tel: +44 1963 442030 Int. fax: +44 1963 440001
E-mail: sales@haynes.co.uk
Website: www.haynes.co.uk

Haynes North America Inc., 861 Lawrence Drive,
Newbury Park, California 91320, USA

Images © Mirrorpix

Creative Director: Kevin Gardner
Designed for Haynes by BrainWave

Printed and bound in the US

When
FOOTBALL *Was*
FOOTBALL

WEST BROMWICH ALBION

A Nostalgic Look at a Century of the Club

David Instone

Contents

Foreword

4 Foreword

6 Having a Ball — 1870-1890

12 Keeping the Winning Habit — 1891-1914

24 A League Title and Winners at Wembley — 1919-1939

36 Happy Days Ahead — 1939-1954

50 Still Hitting the Right Notes — 1954-1963

66 Chasing the BIG Prizes — 1963-1967

88 All Dressed Up for the Big Day — 1968-1970

118 A Changing of the Guard — 1971-1975

132 A Vintage Era — 1976-1982

176 Torrid Times — 1983-1992

190 On the Way Back! — 1993-2002

I wasn't born in West Bromwich. I wasn't even born in England. But The Hawthorns is my football home … it always has been and always will be.

I was 16 when I left behind my beloved Wales and tried my luck with a club who had just won the FA Cup and finished runners-up in the First Division. Eighteen years and some 360 first-team matches later, I was still there, a Baggie through and through, hooked for life. And we didn't do too badly along the way.

My generation won the FA Cup and, as skipper, I was lucky enough to get my hands on that treasured silverware first. That was 1968 – a time when our supporters used to joke that they had season tickets at Wembley. Well, we also went there in 1967 and 1970 for League Cup finals and won that competition in 1965–66 in the last of the two-legged finals.

Throw in the club's first forays in European competition, a defeat in an FA Cup semi-final and all those trips round the world – and it's obvious why those of us who were involved regard ourselves as privileged to have been a part of it.

On a personal level, I was delighted to see how well this book covers my time at my club.

Don't let footballers kid you they don't read newspapers. Of course they do. I had good mates in the press box and, at the same time, always appreciated the skills of the photographers, sitting or lying at pitch-side in all weathers and proving the saying that a good picture is worth a thousand words.

This quality publication has brought back so many happy memories for me … the cups, the near misses, the trips and the laughs. Thank goodness the staff at the *Daily Mirror* not only keep fabulous archives but are prepared to go in there and dust off some of the treasures they hold for the enjoyment of supporters.

There are pictures in here that I thought had been lost forever. What about those wonderful shots, for example, from our victorious dressing rooms at Wembley and Maine Road in 1968! Where on earth have they suddenly reappeared from?

Somewhere, my son has a picture of me swinging my fist back to land one on an opponent during a brawl on our tour of East Africa in 1968. So, if ever the *Mirror* plan to do a second volume …

In the meantime, savour every step of this one. What a brilliant journey it provides, through Albion's glorious history.

Graham Williams

Having a Ball
1870-1890

Unmistakably Albion … one of the early team pictures of a side who emerged quickly in the 1870s and 1880s as a force to be reckoned with.

1879 West Bromwich Strollers are formed thanks to the determination of a group of lads from George Salter Spring Works. **1881** The name Albion, marking the district of West Bromwich the youngsters were from, replaces 'Strollers'. **1882** Albion hammer Coseley 26-0 in the Birmingham Senior Cup – still the club's highest ever victory; fighting breaks out as Albion and Aston Villa have their first face to face – a Staffordshire Cup tie at Perry Barr. **1883** Albion and Wolves kick off their 130-year rivalry by meeting for the first time (in the Birmingham Senior Cup); Wednesbury Town triumph 2-0 in Albion's first FA Cup tie; Albion beat Stoke to lift their first silverware, the Staffordshire Cup; goalkeeper Bob Roberts becomes the club's first international footballer. **1886** Albion become the first Midlands club to reach the FA Cup final, which they lose in a replay to Blackburn. **1887** Albion suffer the pain of another FA Cup final defeat – this time against local rivals Villa. **1888** Third-time-lucky Albion win the cup by beating Preston's 'Invincibles' at the Oval, and subsequently contest the 'Championship of the UK' and 'Championship of the World' match with Scottish club Renton; as one of the 12 founder members, Albion win 2-0 at Stoke in their first Football League game.

Getting the Ball Rolling

Life was not easy for the group of working-class lads who kicked things off by deciding to emulate the winter fun they heard their counterparts were enjoying elsewhere in the Black Country. The friends worked together at West Bromwich's George Salter Spring Works, and had to walk several miles into Wednesbury to buy their first ball as no shop in their home town stocked them. Each of them chucked sixpence into the kitty and dug deep for twopence a week as subscription to a club known initially as West Bromwich Strollers. For their kickabouts, they descended on Cooper's Hill, near one of the town's main features, Dartmouth Park. Black Lake Victoria and Bullock's Club are among the first known opponents for a side who were to indulge in some early 'ground-hopping' in search of a better pitch, and who were soon watched by crowds numbering several hundred.

ABOVE LEFT: Among Albion's early star players was Bob Roberts. Tall, powerful and kitted out in size 13 boots, he was a formidable sight, although far from being the most gifted member of the group. He was, though, more than a little versatile. Initially a left-back, he soon switched to playing in goal and became the club's first international. The 'Prince of Goalkeepers' played three times for England.

ABOVE RIGHT: Not a bad three bobsworth!

Albion players and officials pictured at the opening of the club's Stoney Lane ground on 5th September 1885. The visitors were Third Lanark Rifle Volunteers, no less. Albion had previously used the Four Acres cricket ground for their home matches.

A Major Force in the Making

Albion had warmed up for the big impact they made in the FA Cup by lifting their first silverware in 1883. They defeated Stoke in the final of the Staffordshire Cup and immediately broadened their horizons by entering the FA Cup for the first time, although their journey was rendered a short one when they lost at home to Wednesbury Town.

Word of their dramatic emergence was growing. Preston North End, the country's top team, were beaten 2-1 in a Boxing Day friendly in front of 3,600 spectators in West Bromwich, and no fewer than 16,393 were present when another northern 'giant', Blackburn Rovers, came south and conquered in an 1884–85 FA Cup quarter-final tie.

There was a Rovers return in 1886. Albion had fortune on their side as they were drawn at home in every round and even played the semi-final at nearby Aston as they were facing Small Heath. That 4-1 derby win counted for little the following month, though, when Blackburn beat Albion 2-0 in a replay at Derby after the original final had ended 0-0 at a packed Kennington Oval.

It was the first time any Midlands club had reached the FA Cup final, and Albion underlined their growing status by winning the Birmingham and Staffordshire Cups that year and setting themselves up for another powerful tilt in the big one in 1886–87.

Sadly, that attempt also ended in heartbreak – this time 2-0 against Aston Villa back at the Oval.

FA Cup final 1886 (replay)

Date & Venue: 10th April 1886 at Derby

Result: Blackburn Rovers 2 West Bromwich Albion 0

Blackburn Rovers: H Arthur, Turner, Suter, Douglas, Forrest, M'Intyre, Walton, Strachan, Brown, Fecitt, J Sowerbutts

West Bromwich Albion: Roberts, H Green, H Bell, E Horton, Perry, Timmins, Woodhall, T Green, Bayliss, Loach, G Bell

Goals: Sowerbutts (26 min), Brown (75 min)

Attendance: 16,144

Captain: Jem Bayliss

Secretary-manager: Tom Smith

(In the original match on 3rd April at the Oval, which was drawn 0-0, Heyes played instead of Walton for Blackburn. Albion fielded the same team.)

FA Cup final 1887

Date & Venue: 2nd April 1887 at the Oval

Result: Aston Villa 2 West Bromwich Albion 0

Aston Villa: Warner, Coulton, Simmonds, Yates, Dawson, Burton, Davis, Brown, Hunter, Vaughan, Hodgetts

West Bromwich Albion: Roberts, H Green, Aldridge, Horton, Perry, Timmins, Woodhall, T Green, Bayliss, Paddock, Pearson

Goals: Hodgetts (54 min), Hunter (88 min)

Attendance: 15,534

Captain: Jem Bayliss

Secretary-manager: Tom Smith

Third Time Lucky – They're Cup Winners

Fast-forward another 12 months from the second of Albion's FA Cup final disappointments and this time the mood was completely different. After defeating Wolves and Stoke in the earlier rounds, Albion upset the form book at the expense of the so-called Preston 'Invincibles' at the Oval.

So confident were the North End players that they cheekily asked to be pictured with the cup before kick-off. It was the nearest they got to carrying it off.

Although Preston were to win the league and cup double the following year, they met their match on a day on which the gates were slammed shut with a capacity 18,904 inside. Preston had a Dr Mills-Roberts as their goalkeeper and the telling incisions in a 2-1 Albion victory came through goals by Jim 'Jem' Bayliss (his 10th in that season's competition) and George 'Spry' Woodall. The club's weekly wage bill at the time was said to be below £10.

FA Cup final 1888

Date & Venue: 24th March 1888 at the Oval

Result: West Bromwich Albion 2 Preston North End 1

West Bromwich Albion: Roberts, Aldridge, H Green, E Horton, Perry, Timmins, Woodhall, Bassett, Bayliss, Pearson, Wilson

Preston North End: Mills-Roberts, Howarth, Holmes, N Ross, Russell, Gordon, J Ross, Goodall, Dewhurst, Drummond, Graham

Goals: Bayliss (20 min), Dewhurst (50 min), Woodhall (83 min)

Attendance: 18,904

Captain: Jem Bayliss

Secretary-manager: Tom Smith

A Crack at the World Title!

Nineteen-year-old inside-forward Billy Bassett was the architect of the shock FA Cup final win over Preston – and made the first goal. His golden day was complete when he heard, amid the celebrations, that he had been selected for his England debut.

He had another taste of competing against players from another country when his club headed north to take on Scottish Cup holders Renton at Hampden Park. The game was billed as the Championship of the United Kingdom but that accolade was extended when Renton's 4-1 victory excited reporters into hailing them as 'champions of the world'.

As FA Cup winners, Albion were an obvious 'pick' when, later in 1888, the Football League was launched. The club were one of 12 founder members and made a successful start when they won 2-0 at Stoke on 8th September, Joe Wilson having the honour of scoring their first goal in the new competition. The margin of their victory meant they were the table's first leaders and they were also triumphant (against Burnley) in the first league game at their sloping Stoney Lane ground, although they were to finish only sixth. Twelve months later they were in the middle of the pack again in fifth place.

–LEGENDS–

Billy Bassett

West Bromwich Albion had the perfect club servant in William Isaiah Bassett, a man who was born in the town and went on to spend more than half a century with the club.

Initially, he was an outstanding player, lining up mainly on the right wing as he stepped up from playing local junior football to include three FA Cup final appearances in a tally of 311 first-team matches – during an era in which teams played many fewer games than they have done in subsequent decades.

His speedy runs, excellent crossing and fierce shooting brought him 77 goals and many, many more of what came to be known, a century or so later, as 'assists'.

Inevitably, he was recognized by England, achieving half of his 16 caps for them against Scotland. He also played three times for the Football League XI, but playing football provided only part of the story of his career.

After hanging up his boots shortly before the turn of the century, Bassett became an Albion director in 1905 and was elected as their chairman three years later – a seat of power this all-time Baggies great held until his death.

Bassett was so highly regarded he was on the Football League management committee from 1930–37 and, in his later years, was also a member of the England international selection committee as well as a JP.

He died, at the age of 68, a few hours before his beloved club – one he had served for the small matter of 51 years – went into their FA Cup semi-final clash with Preston North End at Highbury in 1937.

Keeping the Winning Habit
1891-1914

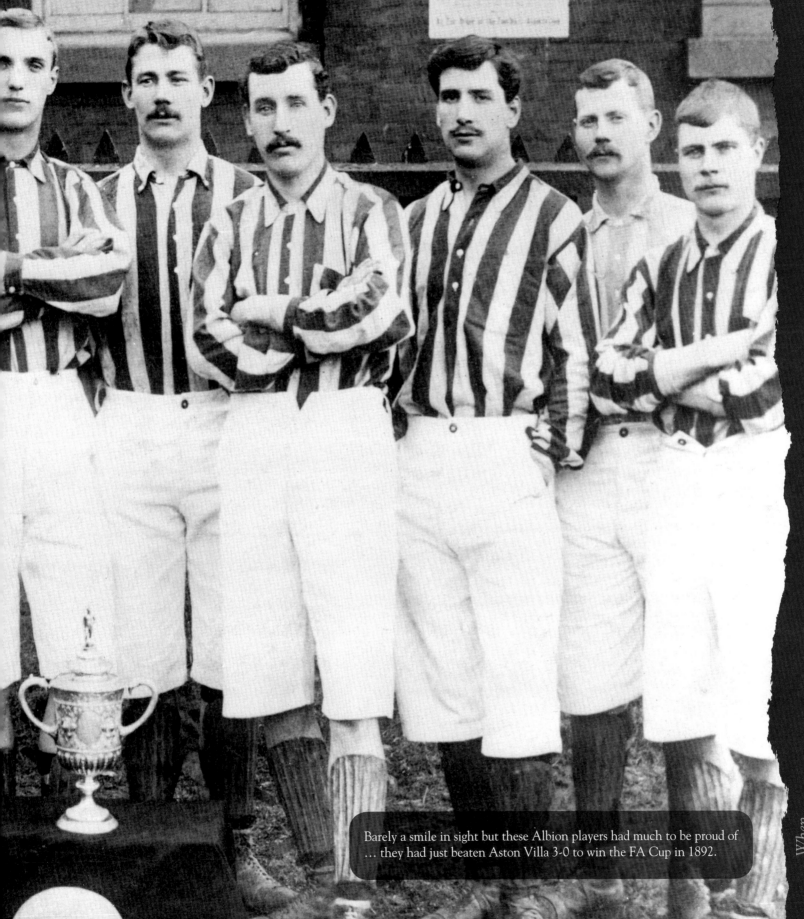

Barely a smile in sight but these Albion players had much to be proud of … they had just beaten Aston Villa 3-0 to win the FA Cup in 1892.

1892 Albion triumph over Aston Villa to win the FA Cup for the second time; Albion set a Football League scoring record by hammering Darwen 12-0. 1895 Revenge gained. This time Villa came out on top in another all-West Midlands FA Cup final meeting, thanks to a first-minute goal. 1900 Albion play their first match at The Hawthorns and draw 1-1 with Derby in front of more than 20,000 on 3rd September. 1901 Albion are relegated for the first time to the Second Division. 1902 A record points total of 55 sees Albion bounce back to the top flight at the first attempt. 1904 The yo-yo existence continues with the wooden spoon and relegation once more; the old stand brought from the club's Stoney League ground to The Hawthorns burns down on Bonfire Night. 1911 Promotion is secured by a Fred Buck penalty that goes through the keeper's legs in the home victory over Huddersfield on the last day of the season. 1912 Albion draw with Barnsley in the FA Cup final at Crystal Palace, only to lose the replay at Sheffield. 1913 The club buy the freehold on The Hawthorns for £5,350, enabling them to finish work on a new grandstand.

The team who were to bring more pride to the Black Country … Albion line-up in the early 1890s.

The Sweetest of Victories

Having registered what still stands as their record FA Cup triumph by winning 10-1 at Chatham in the 1888–89 quarter-final, only to lose at the next hurdle to the Preston side who were destined to become double winners, Albion were beaten semi-finalists again in 1890–91. This was an unhappy season in which they finished bottom of the league – a fate that thankfully did not spell relegation in those days.

They were 12th again in 1891–92, albeit now in a table comprising 14 teams, but covered themselves in FA Cup glory once more along the way. Their run kicked off with a narrow success at Old Westminsters, but was best known for the fact they needed three games to get past Nottingham Forest in the semi-final. Curiously, after 1-1 draws at both Molineux and the County Ground, Derby, they cut loose to thrash the East Midlanders 6-2 back in Wolverhampton.

Invigorated by that scalp, Albion set off for the capital with a relish, which is more than some expected them to do. One Villa fan supposedly wrote to the *Birmingham Gazette* to say that the final was a waste of money and time as his side had already won 3-1 and 5-0 in that season's league clashes.

But this was one of those memorable, unpredictable occasions, as Albion overpowered their neighbours 3-0 in the last final to be played at the Oval. Billy Bassett, described in despatches as 'a master winger', created the first two goals for Alf Geddes (the scorer of a semi-final hat-trick) and Sammy Nicholls, before a spectacular 25-yarder from John 'Baldy' Reynolds killed the game off.

With the season's showpiece staged in mid-March back then, Albion followed up their lifting of the cup for the second time by routing Darwen 12-0 soon after their league programme resumed. It still stands as a record top-flight victory, although Nottingham Forest equalled it in 1909, against Leicester Fosse.

The ball with which Albion overpowered arch-rivals Villa to win the FA Cup for the second time.

FA Cup final 1892

Date & Venue: 19th March 1892 at the Oval

Result: West Bromwich Albion 3 Aston Villa 0

West Bromwich Albion: Reader, Nicholson, McCulloch, Reynolds, C Perry, Groves, Bassett, McLeod, Nicholls, Pearson, Geddes

Aston Villa: Warner, Evans, Cox, H Devey, Cowan, Baird, Athersmith, J Devey, Dickson, Hodgetts, Campbell

Goals: Geddes (4 min), Nicholls (25 min), Reynolds (65 min)

Attendance: 32,710

Captain: Charlie Perry

Secretary-manager: Louis Ford

The Baggies struck out in search of silverware again in the mid-1890s, and came incredibly close to getting their hands on some. They beat Small Heath (the original name for Birmingham City) and Wolves in another memorable FA Cup run, only to lose to an early goal against other local rivals, Aston Villa, in the first final to be played at Crystal Palace. A bumper crowd of nearly 43,000 saw this narrow 1895 eclipse in Albion's fifth final appearance in 10 years, but the side clicked in dramatic fashion only two days later, when they beat Sheffield Wednesday 6-0 to ensure they avoided relegation for the first time.

 They were struggling again 12 months later, though, and stayed up only by virtue of winning two and drawing one of their 'Test' matches – a sort of end-of-season play-off also involving Second Division duo Liverpool and Manchester City, and First Division bottom club Small Heath.

Revenge of the Villa

1895 FA Cup final

Date & Venue: 20th April 1895 at Crystal Palace

Result: Aston Villa 1 West Bromwich Albion 0

Aston Villa: Wilkes, Spencer, Walford, Reynolds, Cowans, Russell, Athersmith, Chatt, Devey, Hodgetts, Smith

West Bromwich Albion: Reader, J Horton, Williams, T Perry, Higgins, Taggart, Bassett, McLeod, Richards, Hutchinson, Banks

Goal: Devey (1 min)

Attendance: 42,652

Captain: Tom Perry

Secretary-manager: Clement Keys

£10 REWARD.

STOLEN!

From the Shop Window of W. Shillcock, Football Outfitter, Newtown Row, Birmingham, between the hour of 9-30 p.m. on Wednesday, the 11th September, and 7-30 a.m., on Thursday, the 12th inst., the

ENGLISH CUP,

the property of Aston Villa F.C. The premises were broken into between the hours named, and the Cup, together with cash in drawer, stolen.

The above Reward will be paid for the recovery of the Cup, or for information as may lead to the conviction of the thieves.

Information to be given to the Chief of Police, or to Mr. W. Shillcock, 73, Newtown Row.

ABOVE: An artist's impression of one of the Albion v Villa final's talking points. Albion centre-half Higgins catches Villa centre-forward Devey with a high challenge.

LEFT: News breaks of the theft of the cup from the W Shillcock sports shop in Birmingham. The disappearance prompted one WAG to say that Villa had lost the prized silverware more than some of their local rivals had won it.

17

Grounds for Optimism

A host of willing hands and even a horse were available (above) when Albion prepared to vacate Stoney Lane and move into their famous Hawthorns home in 1900. The new arena took its name from the fact that throstles (the local name for thrushes) inhabited hawthorn bushes in the area. Derby County were the first visitors on 3rd September, when local dignitaries were well to the fore for the photographers' visit (below).

The West Bromwich Albion Football Club, Ltd.

INCORPORATED UNDER THE COMPANIES ACTS 1862 to 1898.

Registered Office: 253, High Street, West Bromwich.

ISSUE OF £3,000 FIRST MORTGAGE DEBENTURES
carrying interest at £5 per cent. per annum.

MORTGAGE DEBENTURE

No. 3   FOR £100. 0. 0.

I. The West Bromwich Albion Football Club Limited (hereinafter called the "Club") will pay to Messrs John Westerfield & Walter James, Macdowell or other the registered holder for the time being hereof (hereinafter referred to as the registered holder) in accordance with the conditions endorsed hereon the sum of one hundred pounds.

II. The Club will in the meantime, or until payment shall be made of the said principal sum in accordance with the conditions endorsed, hereon, pay to the registered holder as aforesaid interest on the said sum of £100. pounds at the rate of £5 per centum per annum, by equal half-yearly payments on the 30th day of September and the 31st day of March in each year, the first of such half-yearly payments, or a proportionate part thereof from the date hereof, to be made on the next of such dates following the date of issue.

III. The Club hereby charges with such payments its undertaking and all its property whatsoever and wheresoever, both present and future, including its uncalled capital and unpaid calls for the time being.

IV. The Club undertakes to pay to a separate account in a bank all its profits from refreshments and refreshment rights, and from advertisements, and also at least one-fifth of its surplus profits after paying a dividend of 5 per cent. upon its shares, into the names of two of its Directors or other persons who shall hold the same in trust for the time being for the holders of the Debentures of this series for the time being outstanding, and shall pay thereout the interest due on such Debentures, and any balance shall go in redemption of Debentures in the order determined by ballot.

V. This Debenture is issued subject to and with the benefit of the conditions endorsed hereon, which are to be deemed part of it.

GIVEN under the COMMON SEAL of the CLUB this   day of   July, 1900.

The Common Seal of the Club was hereunto duly affixed pursuant to a Resolution of the Board in the presence of

Directors: H Kay, Henry Howell

Secretary: Frank P. Heaven

Fund-raising early 20th-century style as Albion looked to their more affluent supporters for investment.

Back on the Cup Trail

Albion might have added more silverware had they not slipped up at the penultimate stage of the FA Cup in 1906–07. Their run was still very much alive after six games – a sequence that included the conquests of Midlands rivals Stoke (at the third attempt), Derby and Notts County.

But Everton, who had knocked Albion out at the first hurdle the previous year, did for them again in unfortunate circumstances at neutral Bolton. 'West Bromwich played well enough in the first half to have made the game safe, with a very little luck,' the *Daily Mirror* correspondent wrote, 'for they were very much the better side.' Respective keepers Stringer (Albion, above picture) and Scott (Everton, left picture) are seen here in the thick of the action. Note that their jerseys in those days were no different to those of their outfield colleagues.

19

West Bromwich Albion Football Club, Ltd.

Winners English Cup 1887-8, 1891-2.   Runners up 1885-6, 1886-7, 1894-5.
Winners Birmingham Cup 1885-6, 1893-4, 1894-5.
Winners Staffordshire Cup 1883-3, 1885-6, 1886-7, 1888-9, 1899-1900, 1901-2, 1902-3.

Winners Birmingham Charity Cup 1899-1900.
Winners Second Division League Championship, 1901-2, 1910-11.
Winners Birmingham and District League Championship 1901-2.

TELEPHONE NO.:
96 WEST BROMWICH.

TELEGRAPHIC ADDRESS:
"FOOTBALL, WEST BROMWICH."

SECRETARY:
FRED. EVERISS.

Ground and Registered Offices:
"THE HAWTHORNS,"
WEST BROMWICH,

November 14th 1911

Mr J.P.Moore,

Dear Sir,

Thanks for your Debenture duly to hand. We have pleasure in forwarding you cheque £5.0.6 in redemption of same with interest.

Your receipt per return will oblige.

Yours truly,

Secretary.

Cheque duly received
with best thanks
Yrs faithfully
James P. Moore

Pre-war Albion – still a Second Division side, remember – didn't advance past the third round of the FA Cup in any of four seasons after their semi-final appearance in 1907. But they made up for that disappointment by getting things very right in the league in 1911.

Going into the final day of the league campaign, Albion could have missed out on promotion but beat Huddersfield through a penalty by little Fred Buck in front of a season's best Hawthorns crowd of 30,135 to secure the title ahead of Bolton and third-placed Chelsea. It was a day of double celebration for the more partisan Baggies fans because Aston Villa, having led the First Division table with a match to go, lost at Liverpool and were pipped to the top-flight crown by Manchester United.

ABOVE: Early documentation relating both to a shareholding transaction involving West Bromwich Albion and the extraordinary influence on the club of the Everiss family. Between them, Fred Everiss and his son Alan served the club for more than 100 years from the late 1890s, largely in the role of secretary, their mammoth Hawthorns' stints overlapping by nearly two decades.

QUALITY CIGARETTES. SERIES F.B 1 - 96.

BOWSER, WEST BROMWICH.   F.B.87.

LEFT & RIGHT: Handsworth-born Joe Bowser, far and away the leading scorer in Albion's 1910–11 title-winning Second Division season with his 22 league goals, had a magnificent Hawthorns career. In 371 competitive games for the club – a tally that would have been much higher but for the outbreak of war – he scored 72 goals and also won one England cap.

–LEGENDS–

Jesse Pennington

Jesse Pennington is one of the truly iconic names in West Bromwich Albion history. Not surprising as, for 44 years up to 1976 and a certain Tony Brown, he stood proudly as the club's record appearance-maker.

Jesse was even born in West Brom – talk about a local boy making good! From his left-back position, he was an inspirational captain, who led Albion to the Second Division title in 1911, into the FA Cup final the following year and, in 1920, to what still stands as their proudest achievement of all time: their one and only League Championship triumph.

Despite the suspension of the league programme during the First World War, he amassed a colossal total of 496 first-team games while at The Hawthorns, the first and last of them against Liverpool. In the league alone, he played 455 times for Albion.

Word of his excellence spread far beyond the Black Country: Pennington won 25 England caps (from 1907 to 1920) – forming a superb full-back partnership with Blackburn Rovers' Bob Crompton in the England team – was a regular in the Football League XI and won various other international honours. True to form, he was seen as a leader in that elite company, too, and had captaincy experience with his country.

In 1969, not before time, he was made a life member of the club – a fitting reward for record-breaking service that also took in a stint as a coach.

One knack he could not claim to have mastered was that of adding goals to his game. Jesse never scored for the club!

He died in September 1970, at the ripe old age of 87.

FOOTBALL –STATS–

Jesse Pennington

Name: Jesse Pennington

Born: West Bromwich, 1883

Died: 1970

Signed: 1903, from Dudley Town

Albion playing career: 1903–22

Clubs: Dudley Town, Aston Villa, Dudley Town, Albion, Oldbury Town, Notts County

Albion appearances: 496

Albion goals: 0

England appearances: 25

Football League XI appearances: 9

Honours: Second Division winner 1910–11, FA Cup finalist 1912, League Championship winner 1919–20

Jesse in 1964 with his England caps and his various medals.

A Cup Run that Went On and On

Albion's status as gallant and renowned FA Cup fighters was underlined once more in 1911–12, when they made their sixth appearance in a final.

Tottenham Hotspur, Leeds City, Sunderland and Fulham were their victims on the way to the last four, at which point Albion's progress became a test of patience.

They needed two bites at the cherry to get past five-times former winners Blackburn Rovers in the semi-final, with some of the drama captured in the two action photos on this page. The sides initially drew 0-0 at Liverpool before a Bob Pailor goal in extra-time gave Albion a 1-0 victory in the replay in Sheffield four days later.

Two matches were also required to settle the final against Barnsley, and there was a sense of grievance at The Hawthorns that Albion, having been held 0-0 in the first meeting at Crystal Palace, had to travel to South Yorkshire for the replay. There, with huge home advantage in Sheffield, Barnsley prevailed, with the only goal coming in extra-time.

FA Cup final 1912

Date & Venue: 28th April 1912 at Bramall Lane, Sheffield

Result: Barnsley 1 West Bromwich Albion 0

Barnsley: Cooper, Downs, Taylor, Glendinning, Bratley, Utley, Bartrop, Tufnell, Lillycrop, Travers, Moore

West Bromwich Albion: Pearson, Cook, Pennington, Baddeley, Buck, McNeal, Jephcott, Wright, Pailor, Bowser, Shearman

Goal: Tufnell (118 min)

Attendance: 38,000

Captain: Jesse Pennington

Secretary-manager: Fred Everiss

(The two teams had been the same for the 0-0 draw between them at Crystal Palace four days earlier, when the attendance was 54,556.)

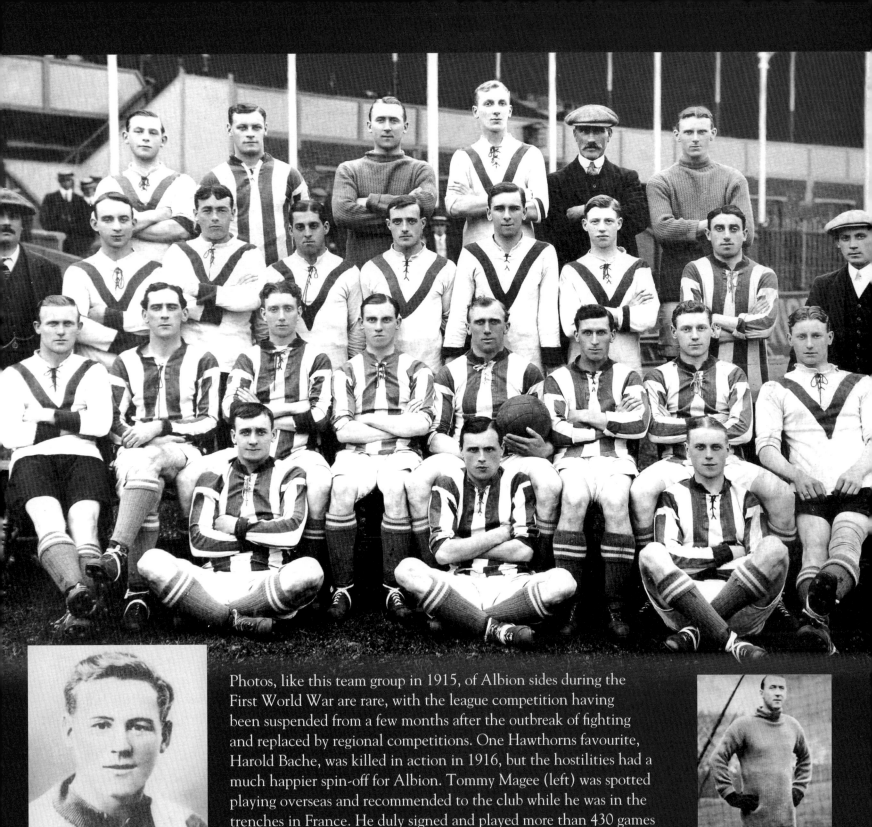

Photos, like this team group in 1915, of Albion sides during the First World War are rare, with the league competition having been suspended from a few months after the outbreak of fighting and replaced by regional competitions. One Hawthorns favourite, Harold Bache, was killed in action in 1916, but the hostilities had a much happier spin-off for Albion. Tommy Magee (left) was spotted playing overseas and recommended to the club while he was in the trenches in France. He duly signed and played more than 430 games for them. Keeper Hubert Pearson (right) was a major figure in the Black Country before and after the conflict, making 377 Albion appearances in total and even scoring twice – both from penalties.

23

A League Title and Winners at Wembley

1919-1939

Trophy winning was a commonplace occurrence at The Hawthorns in decades gone by! So were the team photographs to celebrate

1920 Albion win the League Championship for the first time – in the first postwar season of league football. **1923** The club's first 50,000-plus home attendance (56,474) witnesses an FA Cup victory against Sunderland. **1925** Albion go close to a second title before being beaten to the prize by Huddersfield; The Hawthorns crowd record falls again as 64,612 watch an FA Cup tie against Aston Villa. **1927** A rapid reversal of fortunes sees Albion finish bottom of the First Division and suffer relegation for the third time. **1928** Jimmy Cookson, having smashed Chesterfield's goals record, becomes the Baggies' highest scorer in a season by netting 38 times in the league. **1929** W G Richardson makes his Albion debut and scores in a 6-1 win over Millwall. **1931** What a double! Albion win the FA Cup and promotion, the latter as runners-up to Everton, and some 150,000 welcome them home with the cup; W G Richardson scores four times in five minutes during a league victory away to West Ham. **1935** Another thrilling FA Cup adventure ends in heartbreak as Sheffield Wednesday beat the Baggies in the final at Wembley. **1937** Albion crash to a 10-3 First Division defeat at Stoke – the equal heaviest in their history; a home FA Cup quarter-final against Arsenal pulls in 64,815 spectators – still a Hawthorns record; the death of Billy Bassett, followed by FA Cup semi-final defeat against Preston at Highbury, leaves The Hawthorns shrouded in gloom. **1938** Albion slip back into the Second Division, and the outbreak of war condemns them to an extended stay out of the top flight.

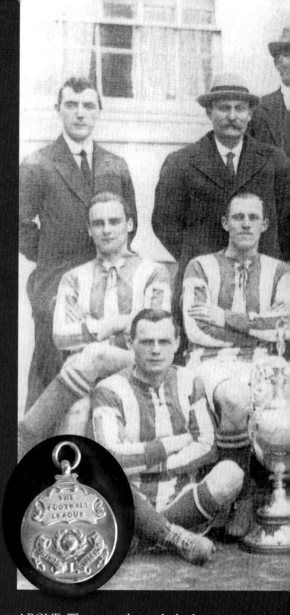

ABOVE: The men who took the league title to The Hawthorns. Back row (from left): W Barber (trainer), H Pearson, W Gopsill (assistant trainer), E Smith (assistant secretary). Third row: F Everiss (secretary), D Nurse (director), A Cook, B Bassett (vice-chairman), H Keys (chairman), C Jephcott, Mr Seymour (director), Lt Col Ely (director). Seated: J Crisp, A Smith, R McNeal, J Pennington, S Bowser, F Morris, H Gregory. Front: J Smith, T Magee, A Bentley, S Richardson. Apart from the League Championship trophy, the photo also shows the Charity Shield, which Albion won in 1920 by beating Tottenham 2-0 away

ABOVE INSET: Goalkeeper Hubert Pearson's championship medal.

West Bromwich Albion F.C.

The Albion News
AND OFFICIAL PROGRAMME.

VOL. XI. (New Series.) No. 43. (Copyright) MAY 1st, 1920.

The Football League.

The League Tables to date are as follows:—

Division I.

Division II.

The Electric Palace, High St., West Bromwich
THE PREMIER PICTURE HOUSE FOR PICTURES AND MUSIC.

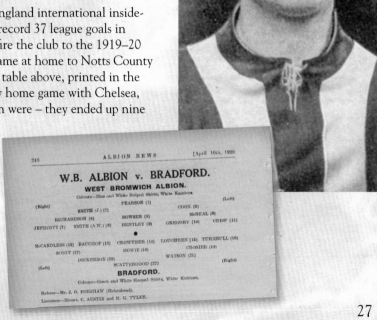

BELOW: Albion's first team weren't the only ones among the silverware immediately after league football resumed following the war. The reserves clicked as well, and were happy to show off their prize for winning the Birmingham and District League.

RIGHT: Fred Morris, the England international inside-forward who scored a then record 37 league goals in an Albion season, helping fire the club to the 1919–20 league title. Five of those came at home to Notts County in the October. The league table above, printed in the programme for the final-day home game with Chelsea, shows how far ahead Albion were – they ended up nine ahead of runners-up Burnley. The title was actually secured three weeks before season's end, at home to Bradford. The teams from that game are shown (right) in the photo of another match-day programme page.

W.B. ALBION v. BRADFORD.

WEST BROMWICH ALBION.

Colours—Blue and White Striped Shirts, White Knickers.

(Right)   (Left)
PEARSON (1)
SMITH (J.) (2)   COOK (3)
RICHARDSON (4)   BOWSER (5)   McNEAL (6)
JEPHCOTT (7)   SMITH (A.W.) (8)   BENTLEY (9)   GREGORY (10)   CRISP (11)

McCANDLESS (12)   BAUCHOP (13)   CROWTHER (14)   LOUGHEEN (15)   TURNBULL (16)
SCOTT (17)   HOWIE (18)   CROSBIE (19)
DICKENSON (20)   WATSON (21)
SCATTERGOOD (22)
(Left)   (Right)

BRADFORD.

Colours—Green and White Hooped Shirts, White Knickers.

Referee—Mr. J. O. FORSHAW (Birkenhead).
Linesmen—Messrs. C. AUSTIN and H. G. TYLER.

–LEGENDS–

Tommy Glidden

Geordie Tommy Glidden gave more than half a century of his life to Albion and served them wonderfully, first as a player and captain, then as a coach, and finally as a shareholder and long-serving director.

He had a special place in supporters' hearts as the man who climbed the steps of Wembley's Royal Box to be presented with the FA Cup after the Baggies had marked their first visit to the stadium by beating Birmingham City in an all-West Midlands final. A few weeks earlier, he had netted the only goal in a tense semi-final against Everton at Old Trafford.

Glidden also led Albion to promotion from the Second Division that season and back to Wembley in 1935 for another Cup final, this time one they lost against Sheffield Wednesday.

His career appearance tally for the Baggies was a colossal 479 and his total of 140 goals have him riding high in the club's all-time scoring charts.

They are statistics that opened the door to some coaching duties after Glidden played his final match in 1936 and left him unlucky never to have won an England cap, although he did figure in an international trial in 1925 and won schoolboy recognition for his country.

He had the opportunity to continue influencing the club's future when he became a shareholder – a position he followed up by serving on the board from 1951 to 1974.

In April 1972, he received a special award to mark his 50-year association with the club but he died just over two years later in West Bromwich, following a heart attack.

His brother Sid was an Albion reserve in the 1920s.

Devon-born George Ashmore leapt from playing junior football one year to performing in goal in the top flight for Albion the year after. He totalled 268 games for the club and is seen showing his aerial agility (left) and his bravery (below), the latter in a game at Hull.

FOOTBALL –STATS–

Tommy Glidden

Name: Tommy Glidden

Born: Coxbridge, Newcastle-on-Tyne, 1902

Died: 1974

Signed: 1922

Albion playing career: 1922–36

Clubs: Albion

Albion appearances: 479

Albion goals: 140

England appearances: 0

Football League XI appearances: 0

Honours: FA Cup winner 1930–31, Second Division winner 1930–31, FA Cup finalist 1935

Brightening a Gloomy Interlude

Having won the title at the start of the decade and then gone close to a second crown until pipped into runners-up position by Huddersfield in 1924–25, Albion's fortunes took a surprise dip.

They were relegated, with Leeds, when finishing bottom of the pile two seasons later, the 7-0 home victory Albion had recorded over Arsenal a few seasons earlier appearing to be a very distant memory.

In the second tier, the Baggies were playing the likes of South Shields and Clapton Orient but fresh hope lay just round the corner. Jimmy Cookson was a defender released by Manchester City, only for Chesterfield to convert him dramatically to a record-breaking forward – and for Albion to pay very close attention …

Cookson signed at The Hawthorns in the summer of 1927 and, in his first season, smashed Freddie Morris' club record by scoring 38 league goals in a campaign, including six in one game against Blackpool (see cutting on the right).

The club still had to endure four seasons of Second Division football, but they were rebuilding to good effect.

SIX FOR COOKSON
West Bromwich Player's Day Out—Leeds First Defeat

Cookson, of West Bromwich, achieved the finest feat in yesterday's games, scoring all six goals against Blackpool.

He shot his first within six minutes of the start, and went on to score five more goals, demoralising the Blackpool defence.

Tuffnell (2) and Williams scored for Blackpool. After being a goal down at the breather, Manchester City found their shooting boots in the second half to win 2—1, and inflict the first defeat on Leeds United.

The visitors opened with a hot attack and Jennings netted for them after fifteen minutes. Five minutes after the interval Johnson equalised, and he was also responsible for the goal which put the visitors ahead.

In beating Reading by 4 to 1 at Bristol, the City scored their fifth successive victory.

Ding-dong play was the feature at Southampton, and the home team's 5—2 victory is not a fair reflection on Oldham's game, which at times was extremely good.

The local "Derby" at Nottingham provided a somewhat scrappy game, Notts County being lucky to lose by the odd goal in three. Barratt and Gibson scored for the Forest, and Mills for the County.

The Wolves again disappointed at Swansea, suffering a 6—1 defeat. McPherson and Fowler both achieved the "hat-trick" for the home side.

Daily

THE DAILY PICTURE PA

No. 8,557   Registered at the G.P.O. as a Newspaper.   SA

FOR TO-DAY'S CUP

ALBION SURVEY THE BATTLE GROU

BIRMINGHAM IN LAST-MINUTE RUN

Pre-match formalities at the Albion v Wolves FA Cup quarter-final late in the winter of 1930–31. It was an unrelenting fight between the Black Country neighbours, with the teams finishing level at The Hawthorns (1-1) before Baggies skipper Tommy Glidden was left with a smile on his face after a 2-1 victory at Molineux in the replay.

FA Cup final 1931

Date & Venue: 24th April 1931 at Wembley

Result: West Bromwich Albion 2 Birmingham City 1

West Bromwich Albion: Pearson, Shaw, Trentham, Magee, W Richardson, Edwards, Glidden, Carter, W G Richardson, Sandford, Wood

Birmingham City: Hibbs, Liddell, Barkas, Cringan, Morrall, Leslie, Briggs, Crosbie, Bradford, Gregg, Curtis

Goals: W G Richardson (25 min), Bradford (59 min), W G Richardson (60 min)

Attendance: 92,406

Captain: Tommy Glidden

Secretary-manager: Fred Everiss

Mirror

H THE LARGEST NET SALE

APRIL 25, 1931   One Penny

INAL

LEFT: Tommy Glidden gets his hands on the cherished silverware from the Duke of Gloucester at a sodden Wembley.

BELOW: Smiles all round as Albion set off on their lap of honour with the cup – back in their possession for the first time in nearly 40 years.

SUNDAY·PICTORIAL

SALE VASTLY IN EXCESS OF ANY OTHER PICTURE PAPER IN THE WORLD

£3,000 MUST-BE-WON CROSSWORD

No. 841   SUNDAY, APRIL 26, 1931   Twopence

EST BROMWICH ALBION WIN THE CUP IN THE RAIN

Albion's previous FA Cup finals had been staged at the likes of the Oval and Crystal Palace; even at Derby and Sheffield United. In 1931, the club and their supporters had a new experience to savour – a day out at Wembley.

In many ways, it was surprising the Baggies had to wait so long to go there, given their past prominence in the competition. But they hadn't reached a final since 1912, so they were by no means certainties to put a winning flourish to a run that had already accounted for Charlton Athletic (at the third time of asking), Tottenham Hotspur, Portsmouth, Wolverhampton Wanderers and Everton.

And the fact that their opponents Birmingham City were a First Division side, unlike themselves, underlined that the task beneath the famous twin towers was a difficult one.

But two goals by the phenomenal W G Richardson saw the Baggies home on a dismal rainy day, his second coming a few seconds after Joe Bradford's equalizer and proving to be the decider.

Albion had no problems scoring goals that season. They finished with 99 in all competitions and had five players – Richardson, Tommy Glidden, Stan Wood, Jimmy Cookson and Joe Carter – in double figures.

So the cup was back in their keeping. And a week and a half after their Wembley celebrations, Albion beat Charlton Athletic 3-2 in front of more than 52,000 at The Hawthorns to become the first club ever to win the FA Cup and promotion in the same season.

Albion's players confidently test Wembley's lush acres on the eve of the 1935 FA Cup final. Checking the height of the crossbar from the stepladder (below inset) is Harold Pearson, who made 303 appearances for the club – 74 fewer than his father Hubert. But the younger man was one up in the international stakes. He played once for England whereas his dad had to withdraw through injury on the only occasion he was selected.

FA Cup final 1935

Date & Venue: 27th April 1935 at Wembley

Result: Sheffield Wednesday 4 West Bromwich Albion 2

Sheffield Wednesday: Brown, Nibloe, Catlin, Sharp, Millership, Burrows, Hooper, Surtees, Palethorpe, Starling, Rimmer

West Bromwich Albion: Pearson, Shaw, Trentham, Murphy, W Richardson, Edwards, Glidden, Carter, W G Richardson, Sandford, Boyes

Goals: Palethorpe (3 min), Boyes (21 min), Hooper (67 min), Sandford (72 min), Rimmer (87 min), Rimmer (90 min)

Attendance: 93,204

Captain: Tommy Glidden

Secretary-manager: Fred Everiss

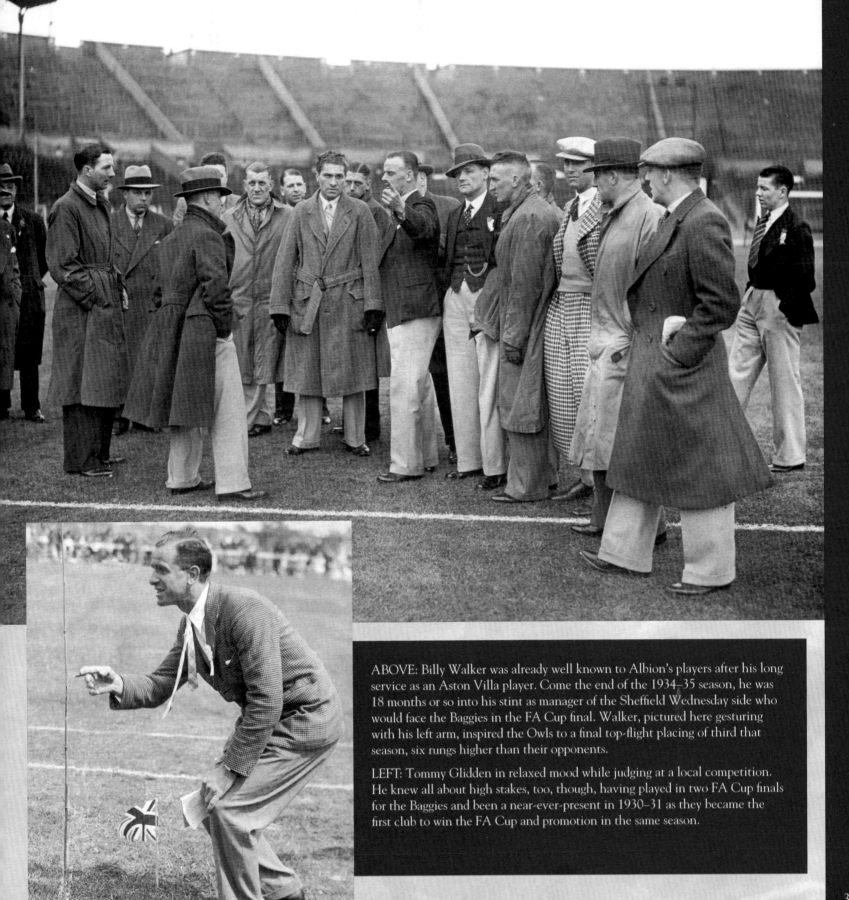

ABOVE: Billy Walker was already well known to Albion's players after his long service as an Aston Villa player. Come the end of the 1934–35 season, he was 18 months or so into his stint as manager of the Sheffield Wednesday side who would face the Baggies in the FA Cup final. Walker, pictured here gesturing with his left arm, inspired the Owls to a final top-flight placing of third that season, six rungs higher than their opponents.

LEFT: Tommy Glidden in relaxed mood while judging at a local competition. He knew all about high stakes, too, though, having played in two FA Cup finals for the Baggies and been a near-ever-present in 1930–31 as they became the first club to win the FA Cup and promotion in the same season.

—'BYE, ARSENAL!

THREE London teams hoped to reach the F A Cup semi-final yesterday One did And that was (hold it !) Millwall, the Third Division giantkillers, who took the mighty Manchester City in their stride and waltzed home by two clear goals, both scored by Mangnall

A sensation ? Just about But what about the end of Arsenal, the favourites, and Spurs ? And the Wolves' great display against Sunderland, who forced them to replay at Roker on Wednesday with a second-half equaliser from Duns ?

This is how they fell—and triumphed :—

Millwall ..	2	Manchester City	0	W.B.A.	3	Arsenal	1
Mangnall 2				W G Richardson,		Bastin	
	Att 42,474, rec £3,381			Mahon 2			
Tottenham	1	Preston N.E.	3		Att 64,815, rec £3,913 (record)		
Duncan		H O'Donnell, F O'Don		Wolverhampton	1	Sunderland	1
		nell Dougall		Jones		Duns	
	Att 71,913, rec £5,714 (record)				Att 57,751 rec £4,278 (record)		

West Bromwich, who claimed one of the three ground records, have equalled another record, that held by Villa and Blackburn, by reaching the semi-final for the thirteenth time They, alone of the five left, have won the Cup since the war

At least London has three teams in the other semi-final—the Amateur Cup Dulwich Hamlet, Leyton and Bromley were successful yesterday And there's just one more bit of Cup news The David v Goliath Scottish Cup-tie, Duns v Motherwell, postponed from the week before, had to be postponed again yesterday.

ARSENAL'S "DOUBLE" WRECKED BY THRILLING ALBION FORWARDS

By P. J. MOSS

West Bromwich A. 3, Arsenal 1

Albion extinguished Arsenal hopes of Cup and League honours for this season and they did it on their merits

Those who saw the splendid football played by the Throstle forwards in that wonderful first quarter of an hour now hope to see something like it at Wembley It was reminiscent of Albion in their best days

Kitchen (Arsenal) makes for goal .. but there's a West Bromwich player moving to challenge him

Five forwards in a line, all going hard defence left to the halves and backs, storming, tearing beautiful football on turf that was a quagmire, a veritable glue-pot

It was the old style football, and it would have beaten any team in the land It could not be kept up and when nature called a halt Arsenal took up the attack, but their forwards could never equal what we had seen before

Anything more thrilling than that first quarter of an hour it would be difficult to imagine The Albion forwards gave us a taste of the football which brought six goals against Sunderland last week

The Arsenal defence was almost overrun and that only one goal, scored by Richardson in the eleventh minute, was registered was rather the Arsenal's luck than Albion's shortcomings

Then the game opened out, and Arsenal had several chances It was the Albion defence's turn to be lucky

Kitchen once beat three men and hit the bar with a terrific shot Just before the interval a foul by Roberts gave Albion their second goal Sandford took the free kick and sent over to Mahon, whose shot struck an Arsenal defender en route

STRANGE GUNNERS

Arsenal man tries to break through with a header against West Bromwich.

Football, as it was recognized and loved, ceased early in 1939–40 and the dark shadow of war stretched across the British Isles. The fitting-out of these youngsters with gas masks was a sure sign that the West Midlands – with all its heavy industry, especially in vehicle manufacture – would become a target for the Luftwaffe bombers.

The 1930s were a dramatic time for Albion, featuring FA Cup and promotion success at the start of the decade, a losing Wembley outing in the middle of it and a defeat in a semi-final in 1937 against Preston. That 4-1 hiding at Highbury came a few hours after the death of the legendary Billy Bassett, the fact that they were three down in half an hour suggesting an element of grief in the dressing room.

It was also a boom period for attendances. One reserve game at home to Aston Villa pulled in 22,372 as the side made history by winning the Central League title three times in a row.

The Hawthorns ground record also fell when Arsenal visited for an FA Cup quarter-final tie on 6th March 1937, and a mammoth 64,815 were squeezed in to enjoy a 3-1 home victory.

After these highs, the club were on something of a low when war broke out. They were relegated in 1938.

W G Richardson wasn't just a phenomenal goalscorer. For many postwar years, he also coached at the club.

–LEGENDS–

W G Richardson

Two goals against Birmingham City in the 1931 FA Cup final underpinned W G Richardson's huge impact at The Hawthorns and ensured he stood for decades as West Bromwich Albion's all-time record marksman.

The northeasterner was a roaring success from the off, scoring 50 times in his first season in Albion's reserves, netting on his senior debut and performing colossal feats in subsequent years.

He hit the decider as the Baggies beat Charlton Athletic to win promotion back to the top flight, netted four times in five minutes in a First Division game at West Ham United later in 1931, scored three in six minutes against Derby County two years later, and was responsible for four of the seven that destroyed a relegation-bound Aston Villa in the middle of the decade.

Surprisingly, Richardson won only one England cap (against Holland in 1935), his peak coming in the months after his second Wembley appearance for Albion, when he scored a club record 40 league and cup goals in a season in 1935–36.

All told, he hit three or more goals in a game 14 times, and continued to run riot through opposition defences during the war. Villa suffered, in particular – he hit five against them in 1943.

Richardson was given the added initial G (for Ginger) to distinguish him from the other W Richardson on Albion's books at the time – a fact that became a talking point when another redhead, Lee Hughes, emerged in the 1990s.

W G later served Albion as trainer-coach and died shortly before his 50th birthday, when he collapsed while playing in a charity match in 1959.

FOOTBALL –STATS–

W G Richardson

Name: W G Richardson

Born: Framwellgate Moor, County Durham, 1909

Died: 1959

Signed: 1929, from Hartlepool United

Albion playing career: 1929–46

Clubs: Hartlepool United, Albion, Derby County (wartime), Walsall (wartime), Shrewsbury Town

Albion appearances: 354

Albion goals: 228

England appearances: 1

Football League XI appearances: 0

Honours: FA Cup winner 1930–31, Second Division promotion winner 1930–31, FA Cup finalist 1935

Happy Days Ahead
1939-1954

Look what we've got! Left-half Ray Barlow, one of Albion's major stars in the 1950s, shows off the FA Cup to starry-eyed youngsters – the prize for the club's win over Preston North End at Wembley in 1954.

1939 W G Richardson becomes the first player to score 200 league goals for Albion when he nets at Sheffield United in January; the club finish a disappointing 10th in the Second Division and a mere 3,109 watch the final game of the season, at home to Norwich; league football is suspended in the autumn because of the outbreak of the Second World War, Harry 'Popeye' Jones' hat-trick against Tottenham on 2nd September being wiped from the record books, along with all league games.

1944 Albion beat Nottingham Forest 6-5 in the final of the Midland War Cup.

1946 Irish international centre-forward Dave Walsh scores in his first six Second Division games for Albion – a Football League record. **1948** Fred Everiss hands over the 'managerial' duties of his secretary-manager role to Jack Smith. **1949** Albion pip Southampton to promotion but miss out on the title by losing their final match, away to Grimsby. **1950** A record Hawthorns league crowd – 60,945 – sees Ronnie Allen score on his debut in a draw against Wolves. **1953** Vic Buckingham succeeds Jesse Carver as manager. **1954** Albion win 3-2 in a thrilling FA Cup final against Preston North End, and are narrowly beaten to the league title by Wolves.

ABOVE: Billy Elliott.

LEFT: Albion players at New Street station en route for an away game in 1948. The train was a common mode of transport in those days.

Billy Elliott, the dynamic right-winger who did so much to keep Hawthorns' morale high during the Second World War and in the years after it. Remarkably, he netted in 11 successive matches in 1941–42. The northeasterner collected his only two England caps during the conflict but may have won many more had he not had the misfortune to be playing at the same time as Stanley Matthews. Cumberland-born Elliott scored 157 goals for Albion in 330 senior games: his record in Football League and FA Cup games standing at 40 from 182 matches. He played 40 league fixtures during Albion's 1948–49 Second Division promotion campaign, contributing seven goals, and was unlucky to have to retire at 32 because of an Achilles injury. He died aged only 47 while on holiday in the Canary Islands, a few months after England's 1966 World Cup triumph.

SOUTHAMPTON FOOTBALL CLUB

PRESIDENT
Rear Admiral Earl Mountbatten of Burma, K.G., P.C., G.M.S.I., G.C.V.O., D.S.O.
CHAIRMAN
W. Penn Barrow, Esq.
DIRECTORS
H. G. Blagrave, Esq., John Corbett, Esq., C. J. Cosgrove, Esq.,
C. F. Hoskins, Esq., R. Jukes, Esq., G. E. H. Prince, Esq., O.B.E., R. J. Stranger, Esq., M.C.
ASST. SECRETARY   SECRETARY & GENERAL MANAGER   TEAM MANAGER
M. BATES   J. R. SARJANTSON   W. DODGIN
Tel. 3408 (After 6 p.m. 68117)

SATURDAY, APRIL 23rd, 1949.   Kick-off 3 p.m.
THE LEAGUE DIVISION II
SOUTHAMPTON
v
WEST BROM. ALBION
NEXT HOME MATCHES
HAMPSHIRE DAY.   SAT., APRIL 30th, 1949.
INTERMEDIATE CUP FINAL, Kick-off 2 p.m.
ALTON TOWN v. RINGWOOD & WELLWORTHY
SENIOR CUP FINAL, Kick-off 3.45 p.m.
ANDOVER v. ROMSEY TOWN

OFFICIAL   2ᴰ   PROGRAMME

The programme front cover from possibly the decisive match in the 1948–49 Second Division promotion race. Albion built on this 1-1 draw at the Dell, where thousands were locked out, and secured their top-flight return by finishing runners-up to Fulham. The Saints fell away and missed out.

A Special Rivalry Brewing

Ray Barlow is denied by Bert Williams as he hurtles in during Albion's 3-2 home league win over Wolves in April 1951. Barlow scored twice and Ronnie Allen once against Baggies' neighbours – and it would not be long before the two teams would dominate the English game. Billy Elliott is pictured to the left while Wolves skipper Billy Wright covers. The no 5 is Bill Shorthouse.

Mixed Fortunes in Manchester

LEFT: Jim Sanders, watched by full-backs Stan Rickaby and Len Millard, touches the ball away to safety in a defeat at Manchester United in 1951.

ABOVE: A happier day for Albion as a hugely talented, young inside-forward named Johnny Nicholls continues his emergence, with one of the goals in a 2-1 win against Manchester City in April 1952.

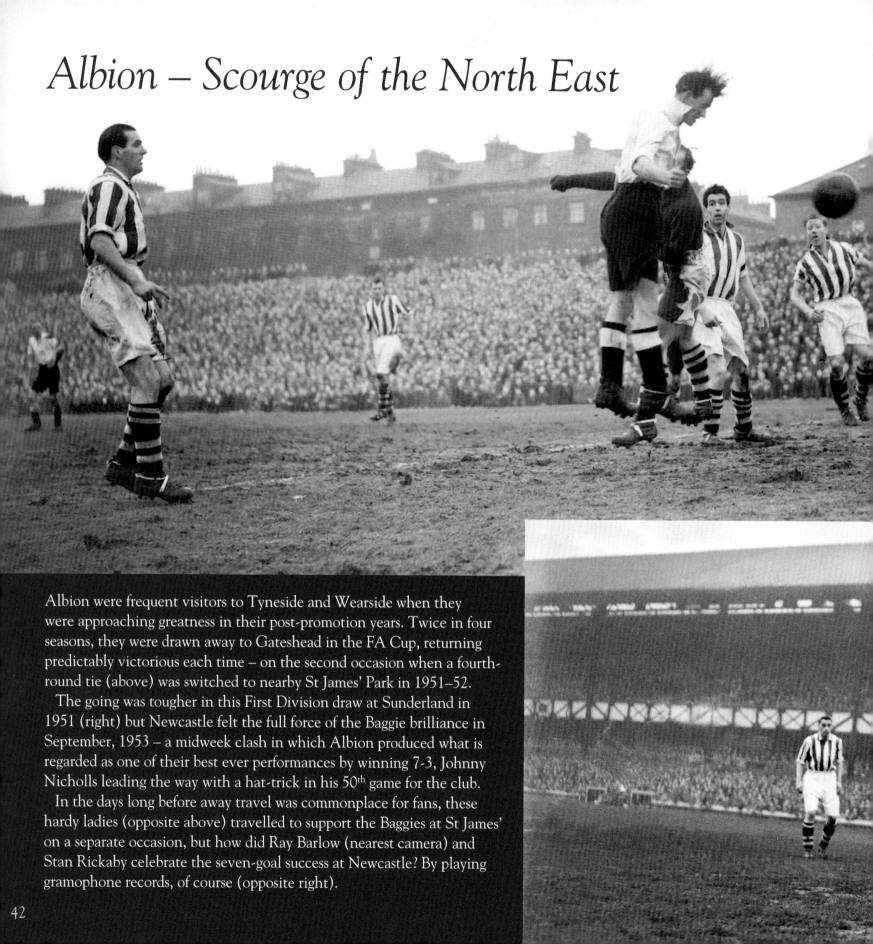

Albion – Scourge of the North East

Albion were frequent visitors to Tyneside and Wearside when they were approaching greatness in their post-promotion years. Twice in four seasons, they were drawn away to Gateshead in the FA Cup, returning predictably victorious each time – on the second occasion when a fourth-round tie (above) was switched to nearby St James' Park in 1951–52.

The going was tougher in this First Division draw at Sunderland in 1951 (right) but Newcastle felt the full force of the Baggie brilliance in September, 1953 – a midweek clash in which Albion produced what is regarded as one of their best ever performances by winning 7-3, Johnny Nicholls leading the way with a hat-trick in his 50th game for the club.

In the days long before away travel was commonplace for fans, these hardy ladies (opposite above) travelled to support the Baggies at St James' on a separate occasion, but how did Ray Barlow (nearest camera) and Stan Rickaby celebrate the seven-goal success at Newcastle? By playing gramophone records, of course (opposite right).

> The crowd just stood and applauded us off at the end.
>
> Johnny Nicholls

43

How else do you prepare for an FA Cup final but with a game of cricket? Ray Barlow (left) and Jimmy Dugdale wait for an edge from the bat of Ronnie Allen, who is dressed in an umpire's coat during this 'down-time' interlude amid the club's Wembley preparations in Reading. Other images on these two pages show Ray Barlow posing for the camera, and covering keeper Norman Heath during Albion's slender 2-1 FA Cup semi-final victory over Third Division Port Vale in the spring of 1954.

–LEGENDS–

Ray Barlow

When no less a man than Bobby Moore says that Ray Barlow was the hero of his youth, and Bobby Robson describes him as one of the greatest players he ever appeared alongside, we realize we are talking about quite a talent …

Unlike the pin-up star of England's World Cup campaign in 1966, the West Bromwich Albion version among the breed of iconic, fair-haired no 6s did not have much of an international career – just the one full cap, in fact, won in a victory over Northern Ireland in the year the Baggies' own cup of joy flowed over.

But the fact he played for the country's B team, the Football League XI, and on tour for the FA representative side on many occasions, underlined what a class act he was. And Hawthorns regulars, from his pomp, realized he was very much part of the backbone of the outstanding Albion line-up of the mid-1950s.

Unusually elegant for a man so tall, he was known for his driving runs into the danger area, one such foray earning a penalty in the Wembley showpiece of 1954 when Barlow was brought down by Preston North End wing-half Tommy Docherty.

Barlow, a quiet man of Wiltshire, was groomed in and around Swindon but recruited by Albion towards the end of the Second World War. And what a force he became!

All told, he played in 449 league and cup matches for the Baggies and scored 36 goals, with some valued wartime service for the club preceding it all.

He was the last survivor of Albion's 1954 cup-winning team and died in March 2012, aged 85.

FOOTBALL –STATS–

Ray Barlow

Name: Ray Barlow

Born: Swindon, 1926

Died: 2012

Signed: 1944

Albion playing career: 1944–62

Clubs: Albion, Birmingham, Stourbridge

Albion appearances: 449

Albion goals: 36

England appearances: 1

Football League XI appearances: 5

Honours: FA Cup winner 1953–54

So Near to the 20th Century's First 'Double'

West Bromwich Albion went close to the league and cup double in 1953–54 in what proved a momentous season for West Midlands football.

Those of us who witnessed the unbelievable promotion battle between Albion and Wolverhampton Wanderers in 2001–02 can only imagine what the tension must have been like almost half a century before.

Albion duly lifted the FA Cup for the first time in 23 years, having added Preston North End's scalp at Wembley to those of Chelsea, Rotherham United, Newcastle United, Tottenham Hotspur and Port Vale, whom they picked off earlier in their goal-filled run.

But they ended the season believing they should really have been league champions as well, as only a late fade-out saw them overhauled by their neighbours.

Albion might have sensed the pendulum swinging against them when they not only lost at Sunderland on the final day of March but saw keeper Norman Heath carried off with a broken neck that was to end his career.

Ray Barlow went in goal at Roker Park, but the beaten side crucially failed to recover quickly, as they also lost by the odd goal three days later at home to Wolves on an afternoon on which both teams were deprived of the services of two key players through calls to the Scotland v England international.

Albion's hopes briefly flickered with a home victory over Manchester City – and the fact that they suffered five defeats in their final seven matches and still finished only four points adrift of the top spot underlined just how close they were to a major slice of football history.

At that time, no club had won the League and FA Cup in the same season in the 20th century.

RIGHT: Albion players celebrate in the Wembley dressing room following their 3-2 FA Cup final victory over Preston in 1954.

FA Cup final 1954

Date & Venue: 1st May 1954 at Wembley

Result: West Bromwich Albion 3 Preston North End 2

West Bromwich Albion: Sanders, Kennedy, Millard, Dudley, Dugdale, Barlow, Griffin, Ryan, Allen, Nicholls, Lee

Preston North End: Thompson, Cunningham, Walton, Docherty, Marston, Forbes, Finney, Foster, Wayman, Baxter, Morrison

Goals: Allen (21 min), Morrison (28 min), Wayman (51 min), Allen (64 min, pen), Griffin (87 min)

Attendance: 99,852

Captain: Len Millard

Manager: Vic Buckingham

Let the celebrations begin! Albion players crowd around the cherished silverware as they set off on their lap of honour a few minutes after Frank Griffin had struck the dramatic late winner against Preston. On the facing page, the main picture shows Ronnie Allen wheeling away in delight after opening the scoring with the first of his two goals. Allen later made it 2-2 by (just) converting one of the most famous penalties in Wembley history. It was gripping stuff – no wonder match-winner Griffin needed to quench his thirst quickly after returning to the dressing room! (inset picture on opposite page).

RIGHT: A handy keepsake from the big day.

WEST BROMWICH ALBION
FOOTBALL CLUB

FOOTBALL ASSOCIATION
CHALLENGE CUP FINAL

CELEBRATION
DINNER

AT

THE CAFÉ ROYAL
REGENT STREET, LONDON, W.1

SATURDAY, 1st MAY, 1954

Still Hitting the Right Notes
1954-1963

Don Howe was a long-time player and manager at Albion but few would remember him as a cabaret act as well! The former England full-back was happy to strum away, though, when he and four team-mates went to visit the convalescing Denis Homer at his home in Dudley. The visit came during the week of the Munich Air Crash in 1958 and was arranged following a letter to the club by the 13-year-old's sister, Jean. Also pictured are (from left) Derek Kevan, Jimmy Dudley, Bobby Robson and Brian Whitehouse.

When **FOOTBALL** *Was* **FOOTBALL**

1954 Ronnie Allen scores a hat-trick as FA Cup holders Albion and league champions Wolves contest the Charity Shield and draw 4-4 in a classic at Molineux. **1957** Having mustered one lowly placing and two mid-table finishes since the golden year of 1954, Albion lose in an FA Cup semi-final replay to Aston Villa at Birmingham City, who also find themselves beaten in the last four; Albion become the first professional club to win in Russia when they beat Dinamo Tbilisi on a summer tour; floodlights are installed and switched on at The Hawthorns for the first time; Manchester City's two visits to the stadium that season result in spectacular 9-2 and 5-1 defeats in the league and FA Cup respectively. **1959** A last-day derby draw at Villa Park means Albion, whose 10 away league victories include Birmingham (6-0) and Portsmouth (6-2), relegate Aston Villa; Vic Buckingham's entertaining six-year spell as manager ends and the Londoner has two subsequent spells with Ajax. **1961** Vic Buckingham's successor, Gordon Clark, leaves after two and a half years in charge and is replaced by Scot Archie Macaulay. **1962** The club are watched by their last 50,000-plus crowd – in an FA Cup quarter-final tie against Tottenham.

An anxious moment as Albion defend in their league game at Stamford Bridge in October 1954. The huge crowd of 67,000 reflected the fact that Chelsea were having an outstanding season that would end with them being crowned champions. Vic Buckingham's side nevertheless battled to a 3-3 draw and were having little trouble scoring goals that autumn. They had another 3-3 draw, with Everton, and beat Leicester 6-4 shortly afterwards.

–LEGENDS–

Len Millard

'Dependable' was the adjective most used to describe the contribution of Len Millard over more than two decades of loyal service at The Hawthorns. 'Fabulous clubman' and 'magnificent servant' are two other tags that sit easily near his name.

Millard actually started his career in junior football as a centre-forward, where he scored two hat-tricks, before switching to half-back. Then, for the final third or so of the club's 1948–49 Second Division promotion-winning season, he replaced Harry Kinsell in the left-back role in which he is so fondly remembered.

This popular local boy – Millard was born just down the road in Coseley – made very good and gave the club lengthy service in wartime matches before making his league debut at Swansea in August 1946.

It was the first of no fewer than 436 league appearances he made for the Baggies, and the 40 outings he had for them in the FA Cup were highlighted by the one at Wembley in 1954 in which he skippered the side to victory over Preston North End. His impact on the final was huge as he kept the legendary Tom Finney quiet throughout the 90 minutes.

Amazingly, Millard missed only 13 games in the first 10 years of postwar football and he was 38 when he had his Football League farewell in a 1-1 draw at Leeds in 1957–58. All told, he played in a colossal 625 matches for his only professional club – one he actually joined as an amateur in 1937.

Sadly, he had a leg amputated in later life and died in 1997, a few days after his 78th birthday.

Len Millard and Johnny Nicholls with the cup, as Albion's players prepare to leave Paddington station for home.

FOOTBALL –STATS–

Len Millard

Name: Len Millard

Born: Coseley, 1919

Died: 1997

Signed: 1937, as an amateur

Albion playing career: 1937–58

Clubs: Bilston Town, Albion

Albion appearances: 477

Albion goals: 7

England appearances: 0

Football League XI appearances: 0

Honours: Second Division runner-up 1948–49, FA Cup winner 1953–54

Ronnie Allen causes havoc with a goal-bound shot in a game against Tottenham at White Hart Lane in the mid-1950s.

Even by the standards of Albion's brilliant 1950s forward line, Ronnie Allen was a special talent: a destructive spearhead in every sense of the phrase.

The statistics say so much … the Stoke-born centre-forward – for that is the position he is most commonly associated with – scored 234 goals in 458 Baggies matches, and stands alone as the one player to have scored in each of the first 20 seasons of league football after the Second World War.

By the end of that span, he was a Crystal Palace player but it is through his heroic deeds as a Hawthorns favourite that he is best known and remembered.

His 208 league goals for Albion constituted a record until Tony Brown went past the figure in 1978, and Allen was the First Division's top marksman in 1954–55 – the season he also bagged a Charity Shield hat-trick away to Wolves – with 27 league goals.

He matched that number in the previous campaign and, for good measure, filled his boots in the FA Cup, including a match-winning brace in the final against Preston.

Allen was a fearsome volleyer of the ball and a penalty-taker supreme. Even in his 60s, he was known to have earned admiration by having the club's 1990s players drooling at his expertise from the spot, even if his shooting no longer packed the same power. Nevertheless, one kick in his dotage is said to have been so hard that it burst the ball.

Given his success in the dugout at Wolves, it's no surprise that the five-times-capped forward also managed Albion. Allen had two stints in charge in the late 1970s (picture below left) and early 1980s, reaching two domestic cup semi-finals in his second spell.

FOOTBALL –STATS–

Ronnie Allen

Name: Ronnie Allen

Born: Fenton, Stoke-on-Trent, 1929

Died: 2001

Signed: 1950, from Port Vale

Albion playing career: 1944–61

Clubs: Port Vale, Albion, Crystal Palace

Albion appearances: 458

Albion goals: 234

England appearances: 5

Football League XI appearances: 1

Honours: FA Cup winner 1953–54

Ronnie Allen's first opportunity as a manager came at, of all places, Wolverhampton Wanderers. And, after restoring top-flight football to Molineux in 1967, he was summoned to a taste of the high life when installed as boss of Athletic Bilbao in 1969 (right).

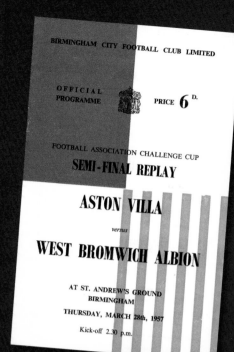

BIRMINGHAM CITY FOOTBALL CLUB LIMITED

OFFICIAL
PROGRAMME   PRICE **6** D.

FOOTBALL ASSOCIATION CHALLENGE CUP

SEMI-FINAL REPLAY

ASTON VILLA

versus

WEST BROMWICH ALBION

AT ST. ANDREW'S GROUND
BIRMINGHAM
THURSDAY, MARCH 28th, 1957
Kick-off 2.30 p.m.

Albion were within a few minutes of a return to Wembley, as they held the upper hand over Aston Villa in a neighbourly FA Cup semi-final in 1957. They led 2-1 with five minutes to go at Molineux, only for Peter McParland to snatch the equalizer and so match the two-goal contribution of the Baggies' Brian Whitehouse. When the tie switched to St Andrew's for the replay, Albion emerged with a hard-luck story and a grievance, Villa's goal leading a charmed life after McParland struck what proved to be the decider. And Albion's mood following their 1-0 defeat was not helped by the fact Ronnie Allen was buffeted by his former Hawthorns team-mate Jimmy Dugdale and had to leave the field badly dazed. Although he briefly returned, his side were left with 10 men when he departed again shortly afterwards. The mood was somewhat less convivial than when players from Albion, Villa and Birmingham congregated in the Second City for a team picture with a difference (above).

Beware The Tank!

> **" *I was always in awe of Derek.*
> *He was a real superstar.* "**
>
> Tony Brown

Derek Kevan, closely marked here, burst on to the scene in the second half of the 1950s and became an icon to a generation of Albion fans. His power and volume of goals are legendary but he uncharacteristically had to take a back seat on this occasion as the scoring in a 3-1 victory at Burnley was done by Dave Burnside (2) and Derek Campbell, the latter (pictured left) captured as he floats home a header.

The Hawthorns
– in Black and White!

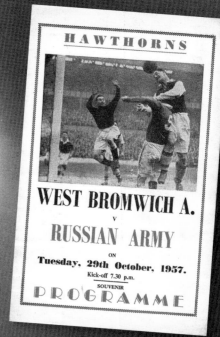

It wasn't only the latest addition to the West Bromwich skyline that lit up the night sky on 29th October 1957 – Albion and Russian side Red Army achieved just the same effect. In the game to mark the official opening of The Hawthorns' first floodlights, which were installed at a cost of £18,000, the Baggies ran out 6-5 winners on a spectacular evening, which was further illuminated at half-time by the legendary ball-juggling skills of Dave Burnside.

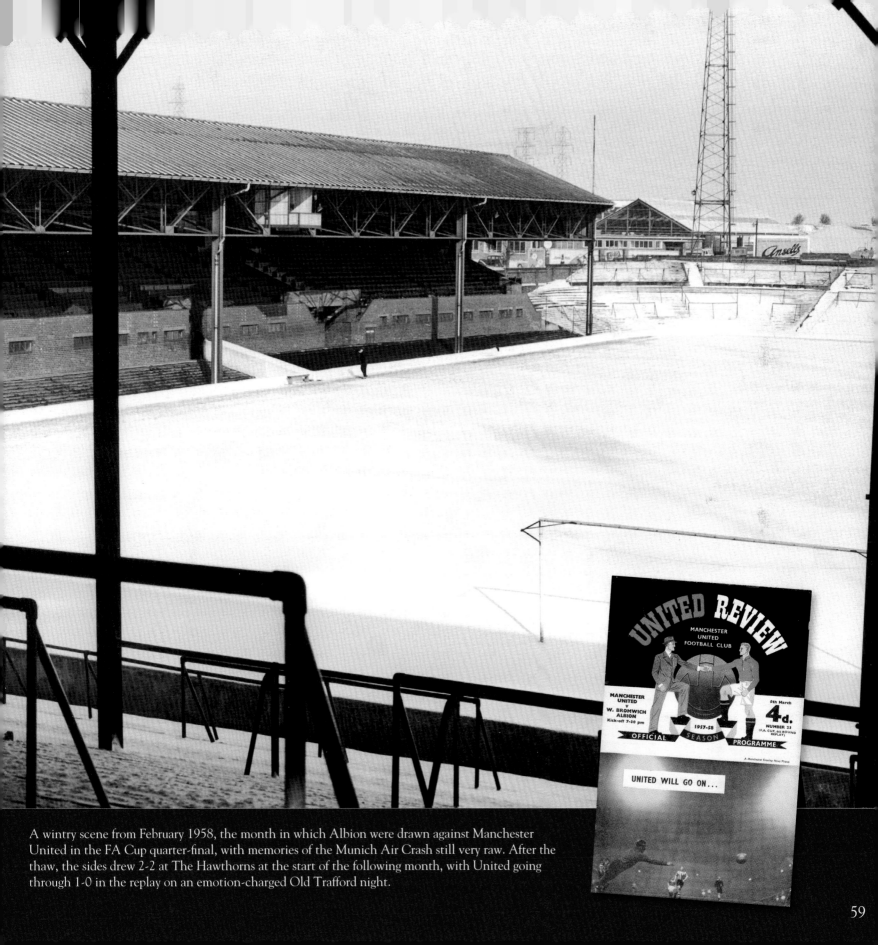

A wintry scene from February 1958, the month in which Albion were drawn against Manchester United in the FA Cup quarter-final, with memories of the Munich Air Crash still very raw. After the thaw, the sides drew 2-2 at The Hawthorns at the start of the following month, with United going through 1-0 in the replay on an emotion-charged Old Trafford night.

Kevan on the Bench!

Albion players went indoors for training in late January 1960, but emerged again successfully to beat Bolton 2-0 in an FA Cup fourth-round tie at The Hawthorns. Also visible, while Derek Kevan does his routines, are Derek Hogg, Dave Burnside, Chuck Drury, Bobby Robson, Jock Wallace, Don Howe and Joe Kennedy.

Excited faces in a then uncovered Birmingham Road End at The Hawthorns in September 1962, at a time when Albion were still an upper-half top-flight team, renowned for playing good football. The mood was particularly bright on this afternoon. Their favourites thrashed Fulham 6-1, with Keith Smith pictured here as he netted one of the two goals with which he ably supported the four-goal Derek Kevan.

Kevan Calling!

BELOW: Derek Kevan and Clive Clark wait to pick up the pieces as Plymouth goalkeeper Dave MacLaren finds himself in trouble during Albion's FA Cup third-round tie at Home Park in January 1963. 'The Tank' scored twice on a day on which the wintry snap meant only a handful of games were played in England. The Baggies hammered their Second Division opponents 5-1 and the freeze meant it was more than two months before they could face Nottingham Forest in round four – a tie they lost in a replay. And they played only two league games in the meantime.

RIGHT: Kevan disembarks after returning from Sweden and the 1958 World Cup finals. The Albion forward scored twice in the tournament and has Don Howe a little behind him on the steps, with Wolves' Bill Slater in between.

Derek Kevan

Name: Derek Kevan

Born: Ripon, 1929

Died: 2013

Signed: 1953, from Bradford Park Avenue

Albion playing career: 1953–63

Clubs: Bradford Park Avenue, Albion, Chelsea, Manchester City, Crystal Palace, Peterborough United, Luton Town, Stockport County, Macclesfield Town, Boston United, Stourbridge

Albion appearances: 291

Albion goals: 173

England appearances: 14

Football League XI appearances: 1

Honours: Fourth Division championship winner 1966–67 (with Stockport)

–LEGENDS– Derek Kevan

What value Albion extracted from the £3,000 they invested in signing Yorkshire powerhouse Derek Kevan in the summer of 1953!

Once his initial clumsiness had been addressed, Vic Buckingham's first Hawthorns signing became a fearsome proposition for opposition defences, his 6ft, 13st frame and rampaging charges making his nickname 'The Tank' utterly appropriate.

He scored both goals in a home victory over Everton on his debut for the club in August 1955, and hit five against the same opponents in the spring of 1960.

Clearly, he was a man with a sense of occasion. Kevan scored a Hawthorns hat-trick against Ipswich in the last of his 262 league matches for the Baggies, and netted along with Duncan Edwards against Scotland on his England debut.

Kevan's goal statistics make remarkable reading … 173 in 291 senior games for Albion and eight in 14 for his country, including two at the 1958 World Cup finals. He was the First Division's joint leading marksman in 1961–62 with 33 – a season he rounded off by banging in two against Fulham and four against Blackpool.

Albion fans were in despair when a bust-up with manager Archie Macaulay led to Kevan's £50,000 departure to Chelsea; he later moved on to Manchester City and wreaked further havoc. In 1963–64, he set a Maine Road record by plundering 30 league goals.

There was still enough left in The Tank's tank to help Stockport to the Fourth Division championship in 1967, by which time he was 32.

A certain band of fans lucky enough to have witnessed his deeds in the Black Country are in no doubt that he is very much one of the Albion greats.

A 1962 goal against Fulham for 'The Tank'.

BELOW: Don signs for a young fan in what is a revealing study of early 1960s transport as well as the football fashion of the day.

BOTTOM: In warmer climes, Don practises his putting in front of (from left) Bobby Robson, Dave Sexton, Alan Ashman and Bertie Mee during 'down time' at the 1970 World Cup in Mexico.

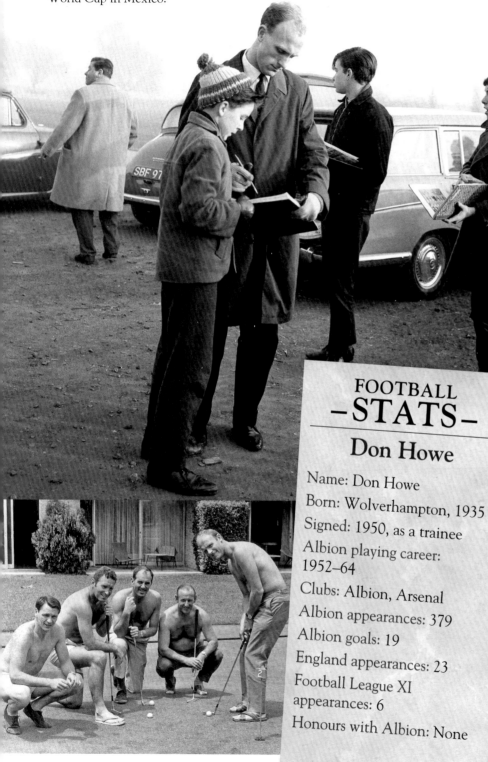

FOOTBALL –STATS–

Don Howe

Name: Don Howe

Born: Wolverhampton, 1935

Signed: 1950, as a trainee

Albion playing career: 1952–64

Clubs: Albion, Arsenal

Albion appearances: 379

Albion goals: 19

England appearances: 23

Football League XI appearances: 6

Honours with Albion: None

–LEGENDS–

Don Howe

For the best part of two decades, Don Howe served West Bromwich Albion – mostly as a resolute, reliable defender and then for almost four full seasons further down the line as their manager. Not bad for a lad Albion snatched from under the noses of Wolves!

Howe went to school in Wolverhampton, the town of his birth, but landed at The Hawthorns in 1950, and had the benefit of learning from some of the thoroughbreds of the Jack Smith and Vic Buckingham eras, before being given his first game in August 1955, in the same side as fellow debutant Derek Kevan. And, once in, Howe took a lot of shifting.

Having graduated just too late for the 1954 FA Cup final, he failed to win any big prizes with the club but made the right-back position his own as he built a tremendous Hawthorns career of 379 first-team appearances.

He played only in the top flight for the club, nearly always in the upper half of it, and appeared in 41 league games out of 42 in the team who finished fourth in 1959–60, only six points behind champions Burnley.

Howe also won 23 England caps, all in a row, to go with his under-23 and B team recognition, and was club captain for several years.

He departed to Arsenal in 1964 and, after a broken leg ended his playing career, he became acclaimed as a coach by helping inspire Bertie Mee's Gunners to the double in 1970–71.

Sadly, Howe's stint as Albion manager was much less successful and he took them down in 1973. But there was one definite plus from his reign: he signed Willie Johnston.

The home side won 2-0. Graham Williams is shown ushering a cross to safety.

Oh Chippy, What Have You Done?

Clive Clark makes the sad, lonely walk to the dressing room after being sent off in the derby against Aston Villa in October 1962.

The impish left-winger was much more sinned against than sinner in his outstanding Albion career, often emerging as a target for robust full-backs with his tricky runs and eye for a goal.

He was often seen with his socks round his ankles, minus shin pads, and demonstrated a bravery on the field that belied an apparent nervousness off it.

In 353 games for the club, he scored no fewer than 98 times, including a brace against his former club, QPR, in the 1967 League Cup final at Wembley. Remarkably, Clark netted goals in every game in that season's competition (eight in seven matches), having also been on target in the second leg of the previous season's final.

If it was any consolation to Clark, Harry Burrows was also sent off in this Villa Park derby – a rare case of two wingers being dismissed. But the result provided no crumbs of comfort.

Chasing the BIG Prizes
1963-1967

Doug Fraser maintains a
determined pursuit of Paddy
Crerand in a Christmas clash
with Manchester United
in 1965. Thanks to a Ray
Crawford goal, Albion
departed from Old Trafford
with a 1-1 draw from their
meeting with the league
champions, and would
themselves win the League
Cup that season. But more
glory was in the offing ...

1963 Jimmy Hagan succeeds Archie Macaulay as Albion manager; Tony Brown scores on his debut in a 2-1 First Division victory at Ipswich; John Kaye becomes the club's record signing at £40,000 when he is recruited from Scunthorpe; Albion players go on strike following a row with Jimmy Hagan. 1964 In a 5-3 home win over Stoke, Bobby Cram becomes the first defender to score a hat-trick for Albion since 1919; Jeff Astle is signed for £25,000 from Notts County and scores twice against Wolves during his home debut. 1965 Graham Lovett becomes Albion's first-used substitute when he goes on for Ken Foggo at Northampton; in the same game, Jeff Astle scores his second hat-trick in a week and the club go to the top of the First Division. 1966 Albion beat West Ham over two legs to win the Football League Cup in the first season they enter it; Hagan's side also finish sixth in the top flight; Albion play in European competition for the first time when they beat DOS Utrecht in the Inter-Cities Fairs Cup. 1967 Having won the last two-legged League Cup final, Albion lose the first to be played at Wembley when they surrender a two-goal lead against Third Division QPR; Hagan is sacked near the end of a season in which relegation is often a major threat.

Here Come the Strikers!

The Hagan Years – Turbulent, Thrilling Times

Walk-out time for Albion's players in the bleak, frozen winter of 1963–64, as they show their disapproval at manager Jimmy Hagan's insistence that they can't wear tracksuit bottoms at any time during training. The players' strike made national headlines and had the TV cameras descending on the club's Spring Road training ground. At the front are keeper Tony Millington (left) and his Welsh international colleague Graham Williams.

Compromise was eventually established between the disciplinarian manager and his squad when it was announced the players would be allowed to wear tracksuit bottoms to warm up in but not during the sessions themselves. There was an ironic twist around the same time when Hagan pressed the wrong pedal while trying to depart the training ground and hurtled 40ft down a steep bank into the adjacent canal. Several of his players saved him from an icy death but, on hearing puffing and panting during the rescue mission, the Sheffield United legend reportedly told one of them: 'You're not fit … extra training this afternoon!'

The Goals Fly In

An early 5-1 victory at Manchester City hinted that the Hagan reign was going to be a goal-filled one – and that point was underlined big time following the arrival of Jeff Astle, 'The King', in the autumn of 1964.

All it took to prise the striker from Notts County was a £25,000 cheque – and the payback started almost immediately with a brace for the new no 9 on his home debut against Wolves. He is pictured (top left) stealing in ahead of Wanderers debutant Graham Hawkins to touch a pull-back from Clive Clark past the out-of-position Fred Davies.

Astle was at it again in the next home game, a 3-0 victory against Liverpool, and would end that season with 11 goals for the club. And he moved up a gear the following season as Albion set the standard in the scoring stakes.

They rattled up no fewer than 119 goals in league and cup games – by far the best in the First Division – and Astle, despite missing 18 games and playing throughout in the no 8 shirt – was responsible for 24 of them.

Among the eye-catching victories were those of 6-2 at home to Stoke and Fulham, while Coventry were despatched 6-1 from The Hawthorns in a League Cup replay. In that tie, 'The King' netted his third hat-trick in just over two months but it was no one-man show.

John Kaye, Hagan's ever-present centre-forward in 1965–66, matched the new boy virtually step for step by banging in 23 of his own and Tony Brown, despite often playing as a right-winger then, was out in front with 27. A fourth man in double figures was Clive Clark (12).

Kaye (2) and Astle were among the marksmen when Leicester were routed 5-1 at The Hawthorns in April (bottom picture, left) during a run of four successive victories. Winger Clark is the man troubling Gordon Banks here a few weeks before the keeper's World Cup final duty.

71

It wasn't all cavalier attacking for Albion under Jimmy Hagan. They had to defend in depth in this mid-1960s game against Burnley, but survived the pressure to leave Turf Moor victorious thanks to a single Ken Foggo goal. The visiting players pictured here are (from left) Terry Simpson, Doug Fraser, Stan Jones and Ray Fairfax. John Kaye (left) bridged the two departments of Albion's side. Bought as a centre-forward and prolific enough in the role in the middle of the decade, he was subsequently converted successfully to a central defender shortly before the club's 1968 FA Cup final triumph.

Scotland v England; Fraser v Robson

Doug Fraser slides in on Bobby Robson in Albion's final defeat of their successful 1965–66 campaign. The club lost this game at Fulham 2-1 but remained unbeaten in their remaining nine games, which included a return to West London for a 3-2 victory over Chelsea. Robson had been a highly impressive performer during his stay at The Hawthorns, playing 257 matches and scoring 61 goals but that appearance figure was dwarfed by the Aberdonian, Fraser, who was one of his successors in the wing-half position.

First-time Entrants Lift the League Cup

Graham Williams sets a skipper's example as he bravely lunges in and blocks a shot from West Ham's Johnny Byrne in the away first leg of the 1966 League Cup final. Ray Potter is the relieved goalkeeper, with Doug Fraser in the background.

BELOW: Although Jimmy Hagan's side were beaten 2-1 at Upton Park, they remained in good spirits for the return, as displayed by these training-ground high jinks involving Bobby Hope and Gerry Howshall and their respective 'jockeys' Graham Williams and John Kaye.

PAGE 30   DAILY MIRROR, Thursday, March 24, 1966

ALBION RACE INTO EUROPE

First-half goal blitz wins League Cup

By PETER INGALL: W.B.A. 4, West Ham 1

(W.B.A. win on aggregate 5-3)

WEST BROMWICH ALBION with a display of high-powered attacking Soccer, became the pride of the Midlands when they brilliantly walked off with the Football League Cup at the Hawthorns last night.

They outclassed a dejected West Ham side in this thrilling second leg of the final to win 5—3 on aggregate.

Their win means that for the first time in five years the Midlands will have a team in European Soccer—The Inter-Cities Fairs Cup—next season.

Excited fans poured on to the field at the end to acclaim their heroes who now join Aston Villa, Birmingham and Leicester City, the other Midlands clubs to win the League Cup.

Albion, a goal down after the first leg, shook West Ham with four brilliant goals in a fantastic 25-minute first-half spell.

The rush started in the ninth minute when right back Bobby Cram thumped a hard cross towards the far post where left winger Clive Clark passed to John Kaye.

The centre forward hit a shot on the turn which screamed past Jim Standen into the net.

Now Albion, playing with their early season sparkle and determination, really turned on the heat.

Kaye, working hard and enjoying the freedom he was getting, missed a great chance just afterwards, volleying the ball over the bar.

But nothing could deter Jimmy Hagan's boys as they tore into the shaky Londoners, who never had a chance to operate their famous defensive blanket.

Albion's second goal came in the 18th minute.

Again Cram lobbed the ball forward and while the Hammers' defenders stood waiting for offside, right winger Tony Brown nipped in to beat Standen, with Clark adding the finishing touch.

Albion grabbed No. 3 in the 27th minute, this time from a Clark header.

WELSH STARLETS PUT WIND UP ENGLAND

By PETER LAKER: England 3 pts, Wales 26

ONCE again, English Rugby is left to pick up the pieces. You could even say that this 13-group international reverse, at Twickenham, was a greater disaster than the seniors' wooden-spoon flop in the championship proper.

Rebuilding begins in the schools. And yesterday we were treated to the so-familiar sight of an England side

The start of a goal-rush . . . West Ham 'keeper Jim Standen dives, but has no chance as centre forward John Kaye's shot flies home for Albion's first goal.

LEAGUE THROW OUT 'BAD BOYS' CLUB

By Mirror Sport Reporter

THE Notts Amateur Football League have expelled Babbington Colliery from its First Division "for the sake of the good name of the League."

behaviour during and after matches.

He added that the expulsion would not prevent the club from reapplying to join the League.

endorsed the League's de-

Results, scorers

LEAGUE CUP
FINAL—2nd Leg
W B A ...... 4 West Ham 1
Kaye 2   Peters
Clark 2   (6-1) 4—8
Williams   (W B A win 5—3 on aggregate)

THIRD DIVISION
Gillingham .... 2 Reading
Backstone   Webb 5,
Brown   Terry

Almost to a man, Albion players of a certain vintage believe that their best ever performance was the one that mercilessly swept West Ham aside in the second leg of the 1966 League Cup final. Some observers have gone as far as to say that the first 45 minutes they produced was one of the most impressive halves of football ever seen at the ground.

The stakes were high at kick-off, with Albion trailing 2-1 from the first leg despite securing the breakthrough early in the second half through Jeff Astle – a lead that was overturned by goals at the other end from Bobby Moore and Johnny Byrne, the latter in stoppage time.

Crucially, Jimmy Hagan was able to call on Bobby Hope for the return, the brilliant midfielder having been out for a month with a knee injury.

And the Scot was well to the fore as Albion stormed, from the off, into opponents who had swamped Cardiff 10-3 in the semi-final. The evening was only nine minutes old when John Kaye rifled the first goal past Jim Standen, who was then beaten when Tony Brown raced on to Bobby Cram's through ball, to bravely head over the advancing keeper.

The goal meant Brown had scored in every round of the tournament, his tally of 10 in it including a hat-trick in the away second leg against Peterborough at the last-four stage.

The home side were rampant and tightened their grip on the cup when Clive Clark nodded home from close range after Kaye had headed Hope's cross back into the danger area.

It was four and as good as all over 10 minutes before the interval when skipper Graham Williams thundered in a left-foot shot following a Hope–Astle link-up.

Albion, who had also beaten Walsall, Leeds, Coventry and Aston Villa in what was their first season of competing in the League Cup, were 5-2 up on aggregate and it hardly mattered that Martin Peters pulled one back 15 minutes before the end.

Twelve years on from the club's last piece of silverware, The Hawthorns' trophy cabinet had a new addition.

The smiles were justified and Albion became headline makers when they ran riot in the second leg.

League Cup final 1966 (second leg)

Date & Venue: 23rd March 1966 at The Hawthorns

Result: West Bromwich Albion 4 West Ham United 1 (5-3 on aggregate)

West Bromwich Albion: Potter, Cram, Fairfax, Fraser, Campbell, Williams, Brown, Astle, Kaye, Hope, Clark

West Ham United: Standen, Burnett, Peters, Bovington, K Brown, Moore, Brabrook, Boyce, Byrne, Hurst, Sissons

Goals: Kaye (9 min), Brown (18 min), Clark (26 min), Williams (35 min), Peters (75 min)

Attendance: 31,925

Captain: Graham Williams

Manager: Jimmy Hagan

(For the first leg, on 9th March, Lovett played instead of Hope for Albion.)

Have we ever previously seen colour team photographs of Albion taken as far from The Hawthorns as this? Both pictures were taken before kick-off on the club's six-game end-of-season tour of South America in the spring of 1966 – a trip that took in Peru, Uruguay, Argentina and Brazil. We're sure it's just coincidence that Graham Lovett has his head bowed on the far right of the back row on the top photo, although he *was* less than happy at twice being sent off during the four-week jaunt. Albion's players were frequent fliers in those days. As well as going to the United States under Jimmy Hagan and then to East Africa, the United States again and Canada with Alan Ashman a few years later, they competed in Europe for the first time in 1966–67 – in the Inter-Cities Fairs Cup. They even twice entered the Anglo-Italian Cup. This and the next three pages are dedicated to travels that were eventful and not always fruitful.

Across the World

Catching some rays by the pool in New York in the 1966 pre-season.

Ray Wilson and reserve keeper Dick Sheppard soaking up some sun at Kilimanjaro in the aftermath of the club's 1968 FA Cup final triumph.

Wish You Were Here – and Here!

FIRST SECTION TEAMS
THE NEW YORKERS OF UNITED STATES
WEST HAM UNITED OF ENGLAND
MUNCHEN 1860 OF W. GERMANY
PORTUGUESA OF BRAZIL
VARESE OF ITALY

FIRST SECTION GAMES

GAME	DATE	TEAMS	GAME TIME
1	May 30 (Sun)	GERMANY vs NEW YORK	4:00 PM
2	June 2 (Wed)	NEW YORK vs ENGLAND	7:30 PM
		GERMANY vs BRAZIL	9:15
3	June 6 (Sun)	GERMANY vs ENGLAND	2:30 PM
		NEW YORK vs BRAZIL	4:15
4	June 9 (Wed)	ITALY vs GERMANY	8:30 PM
5	June 13 (Sun)	NEW YORK vs ITALY	2:30 PM
		GERMANY vs BRAZIL	4:15
6	June 16 (Wed)	ENGLAND vs BRAZIL (SHEA)	8:30 PM
		ITALY vs GERMANY	(CHICAGO)
7	June 20 (Sun)	ITALY vs BRAZIL	2:30 PM
		NEW YORK vs ENGLAND	4:15
8	June 23 (Wed)	ENGLAND vs ITALY	8:30 PM
9	June 28 (Mon)	ITALY vs NEW YORK	7:30 PM
		ENGLAND vs BRAZIL	9:15

CHAMPIONSHIP PLAYOFFS
First and Second Section Winners
AUGUST 1 (SUN. 3 PM) AND AUGUST 4 (WED. 8:30 PM)

SECOND SECTION TEAMS
KILMARNOCK OF SCOTLAND
W. BROMWICH ALBION OF ENGLAND
POLONIA BYTOM OF POLAND
FERENCVAROS OF HUNGARY

SECOND SECTION GAMES

GAME	DATE	TEAMS	GAME TIME
10	July 4 (Sun)	HUNGARY vs SCOTLAND	7:40 PM
11	July 7 (Wed)	ENGLAND vs SCOTLAND	8:30 PM
		HUNGARY vs POLAND	(CHICAGO)
12	July 11 (Sun)	SCOTLAND vs POLAND	2:30 PM
		ENGLAND vs HUNGARY	4:15
13	July 14 (Wed)	ENGLAND vs POLAND	8:30 PM
14	July 18 (Sun)	POLAND vs HUNGARY	2:30 PM
		SCOTLAND vs ENGLAND	4:15
15	July 21 (Wed)	SCOTLAND vs POLAND	7:30 PM
		HUNGARY vs ENGLAND	9:15
16	July 25 (Sun)	ENGLAND vs POLAND	2:30 PM
		SCOTLAND vs HUNGARY	4:15

(Jurisdiction — USSFA)

AMERICAN CHALLENGE CUP
1965 I.S.L. Champion vs Dukla of Czechoslovakia
(Dukla 1961-62-63-64 Challenge Cup Winner)
AUGUST 8 (SUN. 3 PM) AND AUGUST 11 (WED. 8:30 PM)

All single games to be preceded by Junior Team preliminaries for Gov. Rockefeller Cup

The complicated schedule for Albion's trip to the United States tournament in 1966, with matches advertised using the names of the countries, rather than the clubs representing them.

European Combat – A Stormy Ride

Bologna and Albion players emerge for the first leg of their Inter-Cities Fairs Cup tie in Italy in February 1967. Jimmy Hagan's side lost 3-0 and went down 3-1 in the second leg. When the club switched to the European Cup Winners' Cup in 1968–69, trouble quickly flared. Their away leg against Bruges (below), which they turned round at home despite a 3-1 defeat in Belgium, ended in a big punch-up after Jeff Astle had been knocked out and stretchered off to hospital. Their visit to Dinamo Bucharest in the next round (below right) ended in a sending-off for winger Ronnie Rees and a major outbreak of violence from the 15,000 crowd. Albion drew 1-1 in Romania and won the return 4-0, only to go out to Dunfermline in the quarter-final.

WILD FANS MAKE IT A MATCH OF TERROR

Rumanian players rescue frightened Albion from brick and bottle barrage

THE BRAWL AT KAMPALA...

● PICTURES TAKEN BY NATION PHOTOGRAPHER CHANDU VASANI

SUNDAY NATION, June 9, 1968 43

● Alan Hartford, West Brom's 17-year-old inside-forward weeps as trainer Stewart Williams escorts him to the touchline after referee Ngaah sent off the youngster in the second half.

● Manager Alan Ashman talks to skipper Graham Williams and Ronnie Rees after the brawling incident in the second half. Joe Kadenge looks on.

An Albion boot swings wildly as Darlin bursts through to score for Vicenza. The game ended in the seventy-seventh minute.

Italians blame Albion for starting brawl

From MIRROR SPORT REPORTER

Venice Sunday

'Fouls Ignored'

SCREEN HAS A COMEBACK DATE WITH YOUNG WALES

By TOM LYONS

SWANS MAY SIGN HOLE

Trouble continued to follow Albion on their travels across the world. Team-mates recall how Asa Hartford, pictured above in action in an Anglo-Italian Cup tie against Cagliari in 1971, was sent off twice in one game on a stormy tour of Africa in 1968. The midfielder (wearing no 10 in the cutting on the left) reportedly returned to the pitch after being dismissed and was ordered off again for joining in a brawl. He was also involved in the clash which led to the abandonment, 14 minutes from time, of an Anglo-Italian tie away to Lanerossi Vicenza in 1970 (right).

The Sunshine Before the Storm

Bobby Cram is beaten in the air as Denis Law scores the third of the five goals by which Manchester United beat Albion on the opening day of the 1966–67 season. Jimmy Hagan's side scored three of their own and had little trouble finding the net. But, despite more cup success, a relegation struggle was to leave the manager's days numbered.

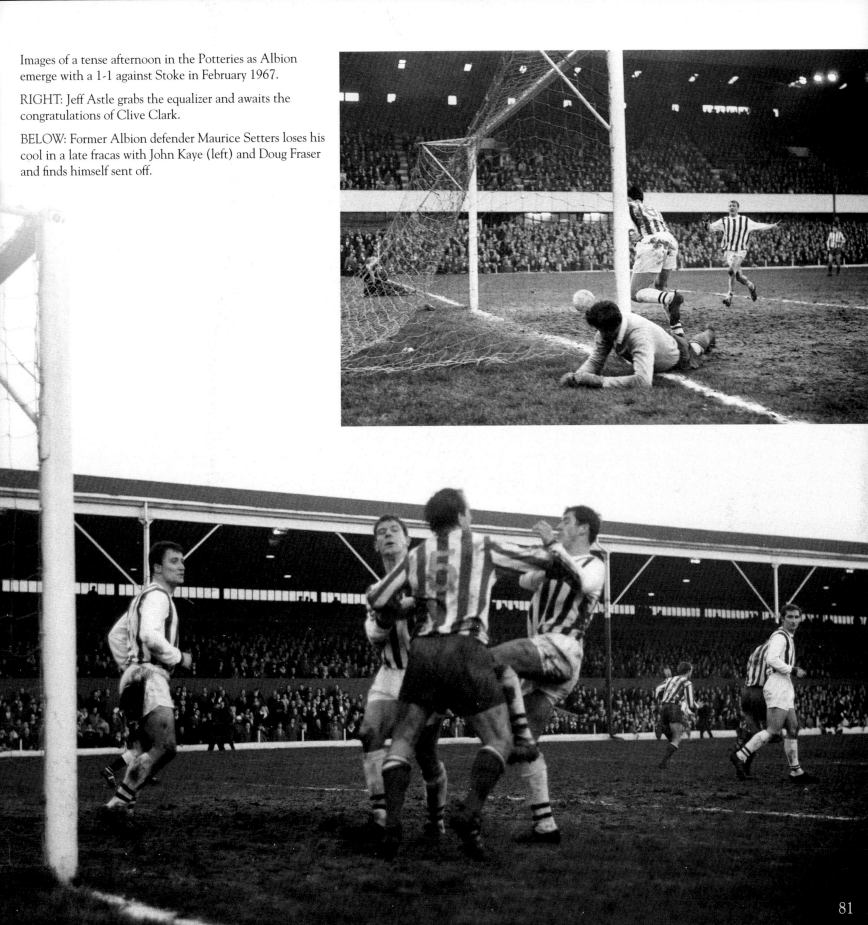

Images of a tense afternoon in the Potteries as Albion emerge with a 1-1 against Stoke in February 1967.

RIGHT: Jeff Astle grabs the equalizer and awaits the congratulations of Clive Clark.

BELOW: Former Albion defender Maurice Setters loses his cool in a late fracas with John Kaye (left) and Doug Fraser and finds himself sent off.

Albion remained the great crowd-pleasers in 1966–67, despite the fact they made it through only one round of the Inter-Cities Cup in their first season in European competition.

Their league form was poor and they hovered around the relegation zone, although they were involved in some high-scoring matches, like Sheffield United (lost 4-3 away), Everton (lost 5-4 away), Fulham (won 5-1 at home), Manchester United (lost 5-3 away and 4-3 at home), Burnley (lost 5-1 away) and Newcastle (won 6-1 at home). In fact their tally of 77 league goals was the fourth highest in the First Division.

Their problem was that the 73 goals they conceded was on the high side as well and it was only an amazing revival from late March that lifted them out of trouble and to a final placing of 13th.

By winning eight and drawing two of their final 11 matches, they spectacularly put things right – but didn't save Jimmy Hagan's job. He was sacked a week and a half before the season's end.

League Cup final 1967

Date & Venue: 4th March 1967 at Wembley

Result: Queens Park Rangers 3 West Bromwich Albion 2

Queens Park Rangers: Springett, Hazell, Langley, Sibley, Hunt, Keen, Lazarus, Sanderson, Allen, Marsh, R Morgan

West Bromwich Albion: Sheppard, Cram, Williams, Collard, Clarke, Fraser, Brown, Astle, Kaye, Hope, Clark

Goals: Clark (7 min), Clark (36 min), Morgan (64 min), Marsh (75 min), Lazarus (84 min)

Attendance: 100,000

Captain: Graham Williams

Manager: Jimmy Hagan

The story of Albion's remarkable League Cup journey in many ways told the story of their bewildering 1966–67 campaign and the final months of the colourful, controversial Jimmy Hagan reign.

Against a backcloth of transfer requests and player dissatisfaction, Albion put inconsistent league form behind them to advance spectacularly in a competition that had a Wembley final for the first time.

Goal-laden successes at home to Aston Villa (6-1) and Manchester City (4-2) set Albion on their way before they faced a difficult night at Third Division Swindon (2-0) and a trip to Second Division Northampton (3-1).

It was then that hapless West Ham, who were no strangers to giving the Baggies a right belting in East London, suffered once more under The Hawthorns' floodlights.

This time it was the semi-final rather than the final as Albion performed brilliantly to win 4-0, Jeff Astle scoring a hat-trick and celebrating one of his goals in the top picture on the facing page. The Hammers twice cut the arrears in the return and threatened another breakthrough (middle photo on facing page), with Dick Sheppard making a fine save while being well protected.

Each time Albion rocked, they pegged back their hosts and so booked their place in the final for the second successive year – an occasion for which they were entitled to feel confident after also hitting the goal trail in the Inter-Cities Fairs Cup. Tony Brown, pictured challenging the air (bottom photo on facing page), hit a hat-trick in this 5-2 win at home to DOS.

Remarkably for a winger, Clive Clark scored in every round of the League Cup, including the opening two goals of what looked like being a one-sided final against his former club, QPR. But the Third Division underdogs, brilliantly inspired by Rodney Marsh, hit back for a totally unforeseen 3-2 victory.

No player reacted better than Jeff Astle, pictured above in action against Arsenal, to the arrival of Alan Ashman as Jimmy Hagan's successor. The former chicken farmer had made his name in management with Carlisle and soon seemed to have 'The King' on an even loftier pedestal. Albion's season nevertheless started uncertainly, and they followed a home defeat against Chelsea with this controversial 3-3 draw against Wolves (left) in their first away game; 'controversial' because Tony Brown confirmed one of the goals went in off his fist!

Are We the Cleanest Team in the League?

Washday high jinks at The Hawthorns in 1967–68 – all part of the more relaxed environment cultivated by Alan Ashman. Pictured checking on the powder requirements are (from left) Graham Williams, John Talbut, Doug Fraser, John Kaye and Bobby Hope.

George Best made his debut against Albion in September 1963 at the age of 17, and made life as difficult for them over the years as he did for all his opponents. This headed goal ushered Alan Ashman's side to a 2-1 First Division defeat at Old Trafford in December 1967, despite John Kaye netting at the other end. This same incident was used as the image for the front cover of this book. The left picture shows Graham Williams trying to keep tabs on the brilliant Ulsterman in the same game.

Back with a Bang

Tony Brown could have joined Manchester City as a teenager but chose Albion because he and his father favoured the homely feel of The Hawthorns. He rarely squandered the chance to remind those at Maine Road what they had missed out on. Over the Christmas period of 1967, Albion brilliantly won home and away against the team who were to scoop that season's title, Brown scoring both in the 3-2 Boxing Day win at home and in this return four days later, when a 2-0 victory even had Alan Ashman's men being talked of as possible championship contenders.

All Dressed Up for the Big Day
1968-1970

What the well-attired fans were wearing at Wembley in 1968 – and pulling from their shopping bags.

1968 Albion kick off their FA Cup campaign with a fortunate, unimpressive draw at Third Division Colchester and win at a canter in the replay; Liverpool are eventually overcome in a titanic three-match quarter-final; local pride is Albion's on semi-final day as spirited Birmingham threaten but fail to land a decisive blow; Jeff Astle scores two hat-tricks in just over 48 hours as Ashman's side put six goals past Manchester United two nights after the semi-final and then beat West Ham 3-1; Astle hits the spectacular Wembley winner to put the result Albion 1 Everton 0 up in lights; FA Cup glory puts Albion back in Europe and they come through controversial ties against Bruges and Dinamo Bucharest. **1969** Albion beat Norwich, Fulham and Arsenal to make excellent progress in their defence of the FA Cup; they then win from behind at Chelsea in the quarter-final, only to surprisingly fall to Second Division Leicester in the semi-final; the European adventure also ends disappointingly – against Dunfermline at the last-eight stage; Colin Suggett, Danny Hegan, Alan Glover and Jim Cumbes arrive in a flurry of major summer spending; the year ends with Albion booking another Wembley visit (their third in just over three years) as they beat Carlisle in the League Cup semi-final. **1970** Tony Brown scores a stunning goal at Sheffield Wednesday as Albion slip out of the FA Cup in the third round; Jeff Astle opens the scoring in the League Cup final against Manchester City, who hit back to win on an awful pitch; Astle goes to Mexico as part of the squad defending England's proudly won World Cup.

> " *I was convinced our Cup run had ended there and then against Colchester.*
>
> John Talbut "

Jeff Astle threatens in Albion's 4-0 FA Cup third-round replay stroll against Colchester at The Hawthorns – a game that fell four days after a scratchy 1-1 draw at Layer Road. In the first meeting, the Third Division club had what appeared to be a perfectly good goal disallowed near the end and John Talbut booted the ball out of the ground in disgust, only to discover that the officials were reprieving the Baggies with a fortunate free-kick decision.

Memories of two games that showed that Ashman's Albion had plenty of resilience about them as they homed in towards their greatest prize of the last 50 years.

ABOVE: John Osborne's defence stand firm in a 0-0 Friday night draw at Tottenham in early March.

BELOW: Dick Sheppard repels danger towards the end of the same month on an afternoon on which Albion hit back from 2-0 down to win 3-2 at Leicester through goals by Clive Clark (2) and Jeff Astle.

91

An Epic Battle

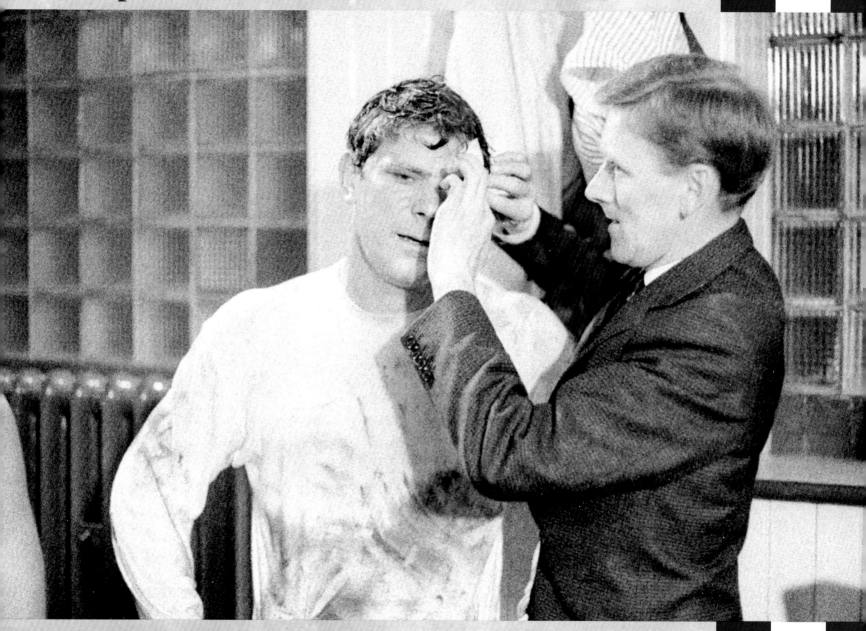

It took three titanic struggles but Albion finally edged mighty Liverpool out of the FA Cup in the spring of 1968. Deadlocked 0-0 at The Hawthorns, despite a great chance for Dick Krzywicki (see photo top left of facing page), and then at 1-1 after extra-time in the replay at Anfield, the teams headed for neutral Maine Road. And Jeff Astle's early breakthrough (top right of facing page) set up a tense 2-1 win that was secured by an outstanding team goal rounded off by Clive Clark. The two scorers are seen celebrating alongside Doug Fraser (opposite) while the above image underlines the bravery of John Kaye, the forward turned defender who played on in the third game despite having a head wound that required a bandage during the game and 12 stitches afterwards.

The Beating of the Blues

A semi-final meeting with Second Division Birmingham at Villa Park – previewed (left) for the *Birmingham Post & Mail* through rival skippers Graham Williams and Ron Wylie – was anything but a straightforward task for Albion, who rode some luck to progress to the final. Jeff Astle's early goal is celebrated (right) with 'Chippy Clark' but the tie was well into the second half before Tony Brown put it to bed with his fourth and last goal of the run. Skipper Williams was at the centre of a bizarre threat before the game, a hoax caller suggesting his wife and children would be kidnapped if Blues lost – a menacing development that ensured a police presence around the family home while the player himself was preparing with the squad at their familiar cup hideaway of Southport. There was no semi-final hangover for Albion … two days later, they thrashed league champions Manchester United 6-3, with Astle scoring what proved the first of two hat-tricks in little over 48 hours and finding time to commiserate with defender Tony Dunne – whether the Irish defender appreciated it or not!

Hope I feel brighter than this come kick-off …

> *Everybody said it would be a cracking final because we were two attacking teams, but it wasn't.*
>
> Jeff Astle

Two of the wounded warriors of Albion's huge Wembley effort.

ABOVE: John Kaye has Jeff Astle for moral support as he ends a run by Everton's Johnny Morrissey.

LEFT: Doug Fraser is helped back to his feet by assistant manager Stuart Williams and Ian Collard. Kaye eventually hobbled off with a knee injury and Dennis Clarke became the first man to go on as a substitute in the FA Cup final.

Albion on the ball against an Everton side who had beaten them home and away in the league in 1967–68 – by a spectacular 6-2 margin at The Hawthorns as recently as the March.

ABOVE: John Kaye in control as Joe Royle challenges.

BELOW: Tony Brown unleashes a shot, with John Hurst trying to block his way.

" *I never want to go through all that again.*

John Osborne on the agonising tension of Cup final day "

FA Cup final 1968
Date & Venue: 18th May 1968 at Wembley
Result: West Bromwich Albion 1 Everton 0
West Bromwich Albion: Osborne, Fraser, Williams, Brown, Talbut, Kaye (Clarke, 91), Lovett, Collard, Astle, Hope, Clark
Everton: West, Wright, Wilson, Kendall, Labone, Harvey, Husband, Ball, Royle, Hurst, Morrissey. Substitute: Kenyon
Goal: Astle (92 min)
Attendance: 100,000
Captain: Graham Williams
Manager: Alan Ashman

–LEGENDS–

Jeff Astle

It takes something special to earn the nickname 'The King'. And a spectacular winner in extra-time of a tight FA Cup final certainly fits into that category.

That sweetest of strikes against Everton 45 years ago was the crowning glory of Jeff Astle's long and magical Albion career; a stay that must seem all the more memorable to Baggies fans given that Wolves manager Stan Cullis scouted the then Notts County forward in a game at Newport just before Jimmy Hagan parted with £25,000 to sign him in 1964.

Astle delivered with two goals against Wolves on his home debut and hardly stopped scoring from that point.

Early in 1965–66, he rattled in two hat-tricks in a week to send his side top of the First Division. Another followed soon after, against Coventry in the middle of the run, that saw the club lift the League Cup. In 1968, Astle bagged two trebles in just over 72 hours.

In-between, he scored three times against West Ham in the semi-final of the League Cup but the 1967–68 campaign brought him his biggest prize.

Astle scored in every round of the FA Cup – in three of the rounds more than once – and, despite his awesome aerial ability, was on such a high that he pinged in the Wembley decider with his unfavoured left foot. Two years later, in a defeat to Manchester City, he became the first man to score in Wembley finals of both the FA Cup and League Cup.

Astle won five England caps, including two at the Mexico World Cup finals, and was named 1968 Midlands Footballer of the Year.

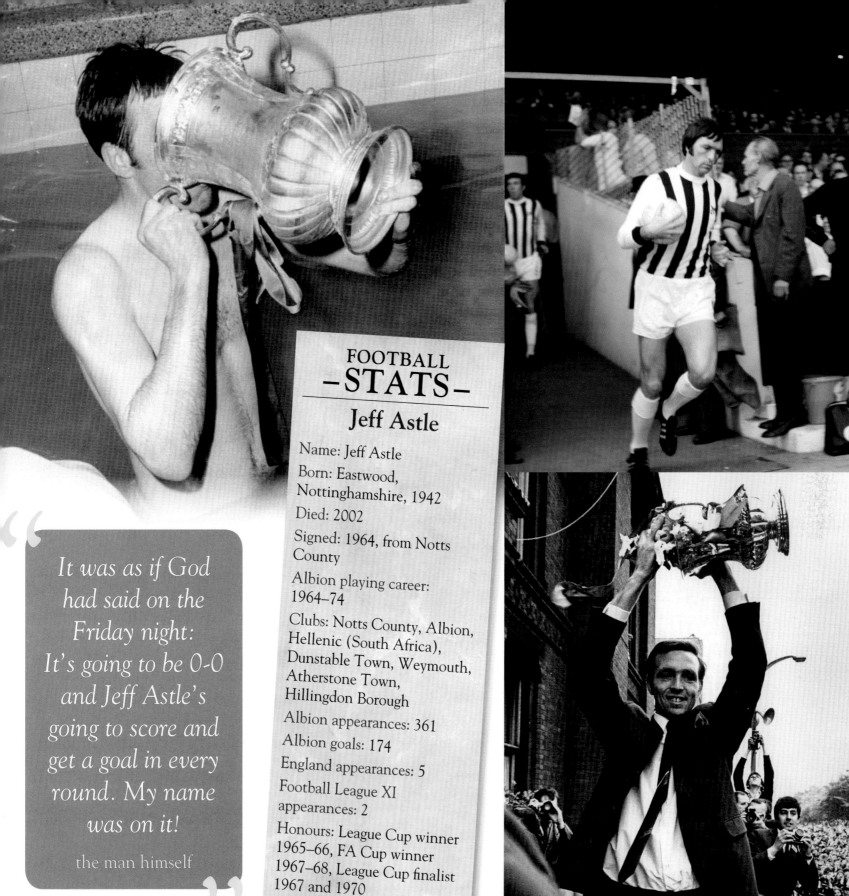

It was as if God had said on the Friday night: It's going to be 0-0 and Jeff Astle's going to score and get a goal in every round. My name was on it!

the man himself

FOOTBALL
–STATS–

Jeff Astle

Name: Jeff Astle

Born: Eastwood, Nottinghamshire, 1942

Died: 2002

Signed: 1964, from Notts County

Albion playing career: 1964–74

Clubs: Notts County, Albion, Hellenic (South Africa), Dunstable Town, Weymouth, Atherstone Town, Hillingdon Borough

Albion appearances: 361

Albion goals: 174

England appearances: 5

Football League XI appearances: 2

Honours: League Cup winner 1965–66, FA Cup winner 1967–68, League Cup finalist 1967 and 1970

–LEGENDS–

Graham Williams

Not only is Graham Williams the last man to have lifted the FA Cup for West Bromwich Albion, he is the first and last captain from the club to wrap his hands round the League Cup and the first man to skipper them into European competition. Not a bad set of entries for the CV … but there is much, much more.

Williams, like several other stalwarts of the 1960s, also played in the first League Cup final to be staged at Wembley and was part, albeit fleetingly, of a side who reached the semi-finals of the 1968–69 FA Cup and the quarter-finals of the same season's European Cup Winners' Cup.

On top of that, he figured in four matches on the way to the 1970 League Cup final and gave 18 years of sterling service to his only Football League club.

A left-winger in his early days, Williams still demonstrated a useful ability to overlap and cross after switching to the left-back post in which he achieved fame at The Hawthorns.

Williams, born in Hellan near Rhyl, won 26 Welsh caps, some of them alongside the unrelated Stuart Williams. And it was after the latter's departure that Graham Williams became a regular in the line-up.

Graham made 40 First Division appearances out of 42 in 1962–63, and basically held down the slot for more than six years at a time when Albion's extraordinary cup exploits meant they could be playing around 60 matches a season.

With 360 outings for the club to his name, it was no surprise when he was asked to do some coaching during the reigns of both Alan Ashman and Don Howe.

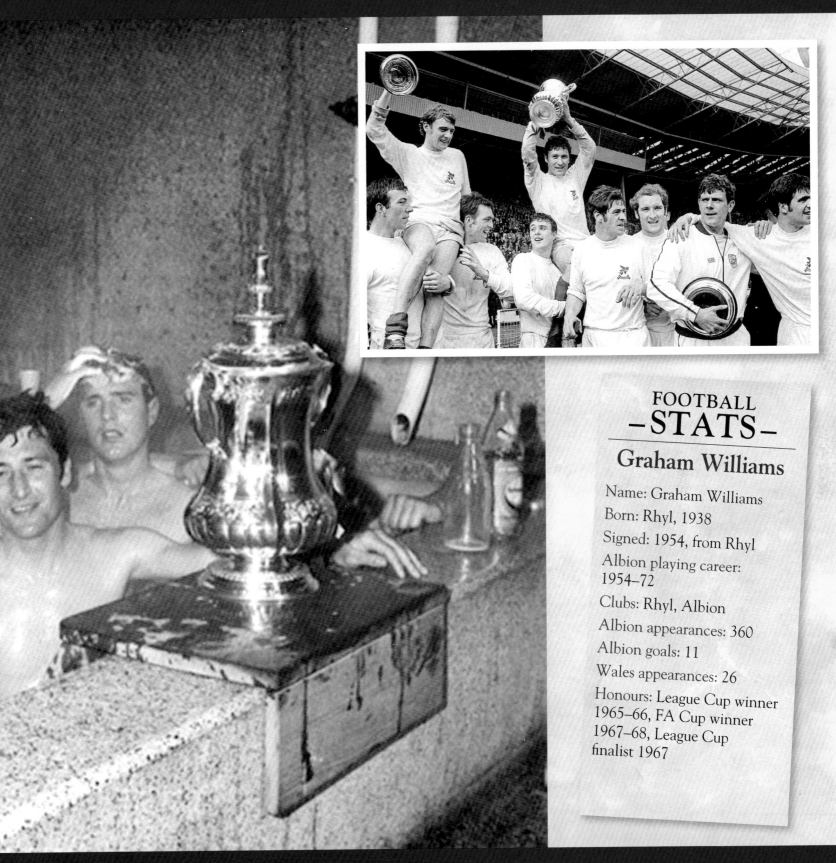

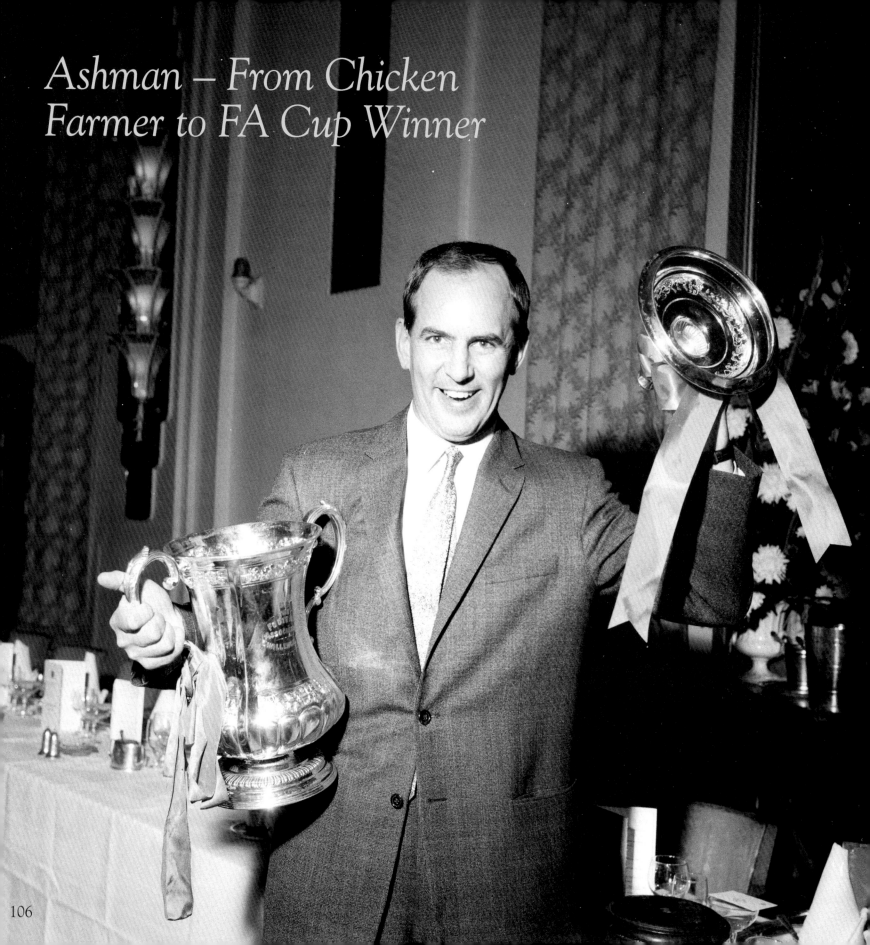

Ashman – From Chicken
Farmer to FA Cup Winner

Home to a Heroes' Reception

Don Everall Travel
CONGRATULATE
WEST BROMWICH ALBION

CUK 525C

One Scot who Didn't Succeed

Bobby Hope – one of the high-class sparks behind Albion's reputation in the 1960s and early 1970s as great entertainers.

Eddie Colquhoun was wearing his Bury club blazer when Jimmy Hagan travelled to Gigg Lane to sign him in 1967. Alas, the defender had the misfortune to be ruled out of the latter stages of Albion's triumphant 1967–68 FA Cup run by an ankle injury suffered at Newcastle on Good Friday, and played only once more for the club.

Two return trips to London at the end of FA Cup-winning year brought mixed fortunes.

ABOVE: The recriminations start as keeper John Osborne remonstrates with John Kaye (left), the grounded Doug Fraser and John Talbut after a Bobby Gould goal in a pre-Christmas defeat at Arsenal.

LEFT: A much happier scene on 28th December as Albion take revenge for their 1967 League Cup final defeat by hammering QPR 4-0 at Loftus Road. Kaye is the man getting a mouthful of ball here as Frank Clarke tries a header.

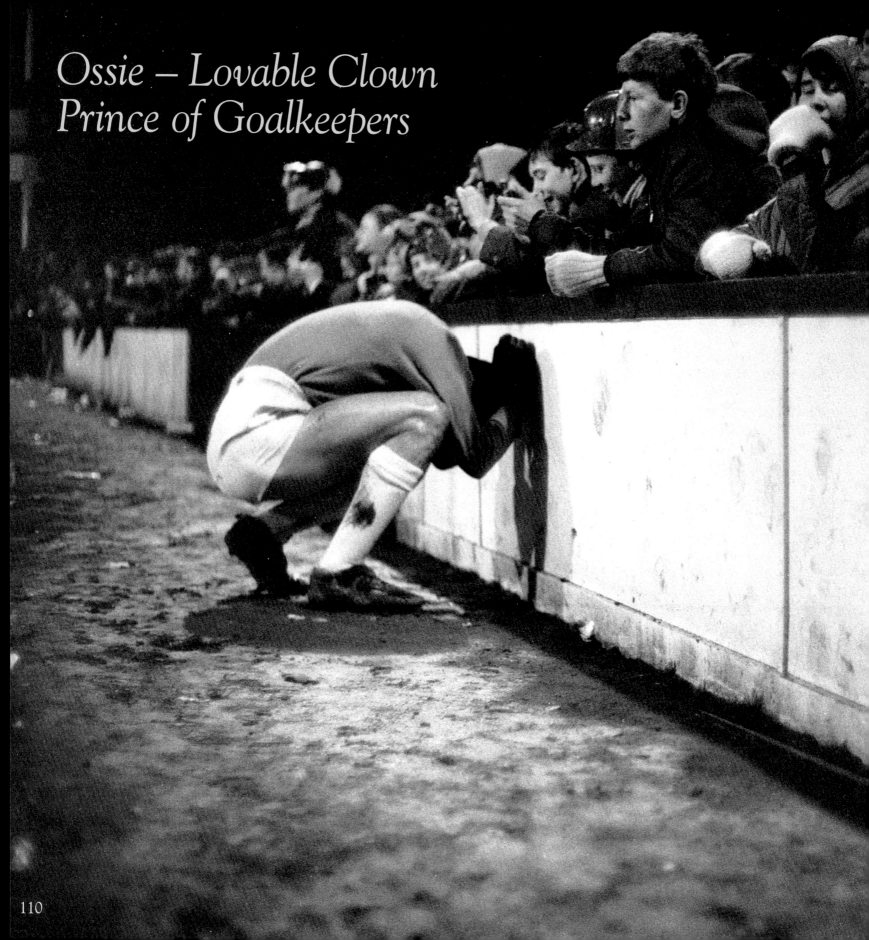

Ossie – Lovable Clown
Prince of Goalkeepers

LEFT: John Osborne crouches behind his goal at Upton Park as Bobby Hope takes – and scores from – a penalty three minutes from time, to give Albion a 3-2 win over West Ham in December 1967.

BELOW: Ossie hangs on at Highbury despite getting a buffeting from Bobby Gould.

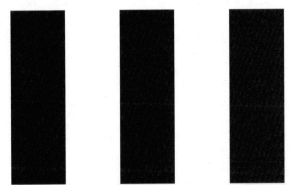

Back on the Cup Trail

Albion's reputation as feared cup fighters remained very much alive in 1968–69. True to form, the FA Cup holders suffered one of those occasional aberrations by losing a League Cup third-round tie at Peterborough but they were more convincing as they entered European competition for the second time. They came through a gruelling, bruising tie against Bruges on the away goals rule and then ultimately made short work of Dinamo Bucharest, following up a 1-1 draw in Romania by running out 4-0 winners in the return. Tony Brown (right) and Graham Lovett (below right) are captured scoring goals on a rare night on which Albion wore their famous all-white cup colours in a home game. The Cup Winners' Cup was shaping up to be something highly promising for the club when they performed well in a 0-0 draw away to Dunfermline in the next round. But the Scots made themselves at home on a raw Hawthorns evening in the second leg, by winning 1-0 through an early goal. Undeterred, Alan Ashman's players were in good heart (below) as they made a spirited start in defence of their proudest possession – the FA Cup.

Albion's players are put through their paces on one of several getaways they made to Southport in the late 1960s (below). The forays were nearly always planned before big cup games – such as the rearranged FA Cup fifth-round victory at home to Arsenal (above). Albion had started their defence of the trophy by beating Norwich at home and Fulham away.

More of that famous Southport spirit! Jeff Astle turns 'horse' for the sake of National Hunt jockey Terry Biddlecombe, who was in the resort at the same time in 1969. Also pictured are (from left) Tony Brown, John Osborne, Bobby Hope and Graham Williams.

The key moments from Albion's gripping Cup quarter-final victory over Chelsea at Stamford Bridge.

ABOVE: Jeff Astle slides home the second-half winner, Tony Brown previously having equalized David Webb's early header.

BELOW: John Osborne saves an injury-time shot by no 4 John Boyle through unorthodox means – and sparks an ugly melee. As the ball briefly spilled loose, a brawl engulfed almost every player on the pitch.

Wembley? I Love it!

Albion made it to Wembley for the third time in four seasons – with a two-leg League Cup final just before that – when they clicked again on the knockout stage in 1969–70. Having missed out on the twin towers in 1969, when they reached an FA Cup semi-final and European Cup Winners' Cup quarter-final, they got it right the following season despite a third-round FA Cup exit at Sheffield Wednesday. In the League Cup, they won at Aston Villa, overcame Ipswich, Bradford City and Leicester at The Hawthorns (the first and last in replays), then hit back from a first-leg deficit to overpower Carlisle 4-2 on aggregate in the semi-final. They even got their noses in front in the final against Manchester City through Jeff Astle – who else? But his early header to Ray Wilson's hanging left-wing centre was equalized by Mike Doyle on the hour and Glyn Pardoe bundled in the winner in extra-time. It was the end of a glorious era in which Albion could lay claim to being the country's genuine cup kings.

ABOVE: Albion fans all dressed up for the big day.

RIGHT: Doug Fraser delivers a throw-in towards City's area from the right. The Wembley pitch became a churned-up mess – a result of the Horse of the Year Show being held on it not long before.

League Cup final 1970

Date & Venue: 7th March 1970 at Wembley

Result: Manchester City 2 West Bromwich Albion 1

Manchester City: Corrigan, Book, Mann, Doyle, Booth, Oakes, Heslop, Bell, Summerbee (Bowyer, 68), Lee, Pardoe

West Bromwich Albion: Osborne, Fraser, Wilson, Brown, Talbut, Kaye, Cantello, Suggett, Astle, Hartford (Krzywicki, 85), Hope

Goals: Astle (5 min), Doyle (60 min), Pardoe (100 min)

Attendance: 97,963

Captain: Doug Fraser

Manager: Alan Ashman

A Changing of the Guard
1971-1975

The Hawthorns landscape changed following the 1970 League Cup final. Popular stalwarts, such as Graham Williams, John Talbut, John Kaye, Doug Fraser and Bobby Hope, were coming towards the end. Clive Clark had already gone and even Jeff Astle was having injury problems. The club's new face is illustrated here by right-back Lyndon Hughes and centre-half John Wile in this 2-2 draw in April 1971, against an Arsenal side destined to win the double that spring.

1971 Albion lose 3-0 at Ipswich in the fourth round of the FA Cup, having crashed 5-0 at Tottenham in the same round of that season's League Cup; a 2-1 victory at Leeds, containing a highly controversial killer goal by Jeff Astle, brings Albion their first away league win in more than 16 months and has a big say in sending the league crown to Arsenal; the win at Elland Road, followed by an entertaining draw at home to Arsenal, isn't enough to spare Alan Ashman the sack; his replacement, Don Howe, starts with two victories, then finds goals increasingly hard to come by as the gloom descends; Asa Hartford's £175,000 move to Leeds collapses when he is found to have a hole in his heart; John Wile, signed from Peterborough, lines up for the first time alongside Alistair Robertson. **1972** Having flirted precariously with the prospect of relegation, Howe's Albion find a rich seam of form to finish 16th, one place higher than the club managed 12 months previously; with another survival battle under way the season after, the club smash their transfer record to lure Willie Johnston south from Rangers for £135,000.

1973 Relegation! Second Division football comes to The Hawthorns for the first time since 1949.
1974 Jeff Astle scores the last of his 174 Albion goals; Hawthorns' gates slip beneath 10,000 as the challenge for promotion remains unconvincing. **1975** Don Howe is sacked after four seasons, the last two of them spent among the Second Division also-rans; in his place, Leeds legend Johnny Giles becomes the club's first player-manager.

ABOVE: Albion were finding Black Country derbies tough going in the late 1960s and early 1970s and slipped to a 4-2 defeat here at The Hawthorns in the second half of 1970–71. George McVitie and Wolves' Derek Parkin are the men doing battle.

John Wile, the last major signing of the Alan Ashman era, pictured during his first day's training midway through 1970–71. The former Peterborough centre-half was to play exactly 500 league games for the club.

Is This the Most Controversial Goal in Albion's History?

Jeff Astle touches into an empty net and so scores the goal that sparked a riot at Elland Road in April 1971. Albion, already 1-0 up on title-chasing Leeds and playing superbly, got lucky when the officials decided that a clearly offside Colin Suggett was not interfering with play. Leeds' defenders stopped and Tony Brown, who had opened the scoring in characteristic fashion, crossed for Astle – also possibly offside – to nudge in. After the pitch had been cleared of irate home spectators, Leeds hit back late on through boyhood Albion fan Allan Clarke but Albion's 2-1 victory was thoroughly deserved and handed the initiative to Arsenal in the championship race. The Gunners were at The Hawthorns the following weekend and were happy to escape with a 2-2 draw, with the fierce exchanges exemplified (left) by this challenge from Frank McLintock on the game's final goalscorer, Tony Brown.

Albion made a limp last stand in the successful and entertaining Alan Ashman era. Following the stirring performances against Leeds and Arsenal, they were well beaten at Newcastle and also in this final league game at Derby (above), although some sparks did fly in their subsequent campaign – still under the manager – in the Anglo-Italian Cup. John Kaye is the man making a firm point with an Italian opponent in The Hawthorns clash with Cagliari (left) shortly before Ashman's sacking, which the manager heard about while on holiday in Greece.

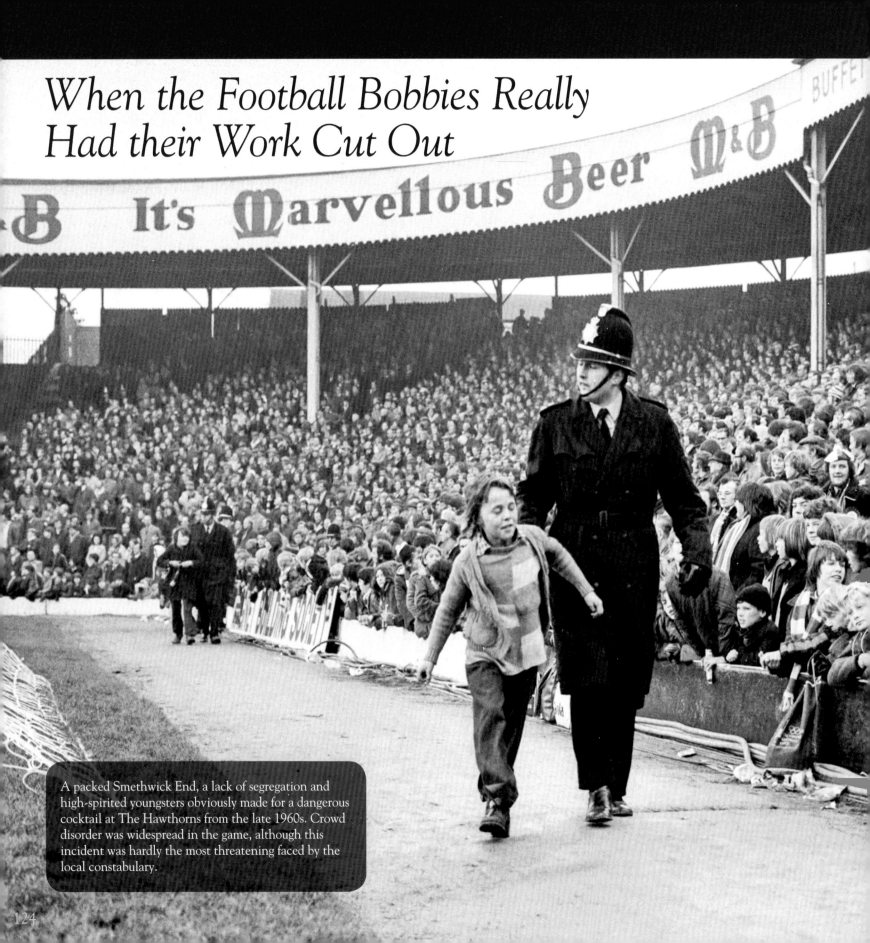

When the Football Bobbies Really Had their Work Cut Out

It's **Marvellous Beer** M&B

A packed Smethwick End, a lack of segregation and high-spirited youngsters obviously made for a dangerous cocktail at The Hawthorns from the late 1960s. Crowd disorder was widespread in the game, although this incident was hardly the most threatening faced by the local constabulary.

The Strange Case of Gordon Nisbet

How many players play their first Football League game as a goalkeeper and then appear in the remaining 700 or so matches of their career outfield? Well, we might not be talking about much more than a one-man 'club'. Gordon Nisbet's debut came between the posts in a 3-1 First Division defeat at Coventry in August 1969 (below). Two and a half years later, in this match at Highbury (above), he was seen for the first time as a first-team right-back. The no 2 is a miserable onlooker, as Arsenal celebrate their second goal in a 2-0 victory against an Albion side who were losing for the seventh game in a row.

Gloom Lifts –
Safety Assured

Albion players kick in before the start of their 2-1 First Division defeat at Manchester City on 1st March 1972 – a game that, unusually, was played on a Wednesday afternoon. Don Howe's side were rallying by then, though, and had won their previous three matches. And they continued to finish the season in some style, with a 4-0 home win over Chelsea (inset right), including an opening goal from no 9 Tony Brown. Yes, that was Albion 4 Chelsea 0!

Albion did more than secure their own survival at the end of 1971–72. They also had a say in the league title race by playing home games against Derby and Leeds in April. John Osborne punches clear here in the 0-0 home draw against Brian Clough's Rams (above), who were crowned champions while on a beach in Majorca. The year 1972, nevertheless, grew more troublesome for Albion, although the club record signing of Willie Johnston (left) from Rangers in the December was an undoubted highlight.

Reprieved thanks to their own major improvement in the final third of 1971–72, Albion were less fortunate the following season. They struggled throughout, even in an FA Cup third-round tie against Second Division Nottingham Forest – which went to four matches. The inset photo shows a fog-shrouded City Ground on the night the first replay between the clubs was abandoned. The rematch was also drawn but the marathon was resolved in Albion's favour when they won 3-1 at neutral Leicester in the fourth meeting of the clubs. The main picture shows Alistair Robertson trying to cut out a shot in the 2-0 defeat at Stoke on the last day of March. Albion won their next two games but then lost the final four to finish bottom of the table.

Second Division Football – the Reality Hits Home

After nearly a quarter of a century of top-flight membership, Albion turned out at some of the game's backwaters in 1973–74: Carlisle, Oxford and Bristol Rovers among them. Six times, including at this turgid late-season goalless draw at Fulham, attendances at their league games dropped below 10,000; thankfully such low attendances all happened when the team was on their travels rather than at The Hawthorns. Don Howe's team often flirted with making a strong challenge for promotion and then fell away – an emphatic double over Aston Villa emerging as crumbs of consolation. Bobby Moore, no less, is the man challenging Tony Brown in this Craven Cottage tussle as Alan Glover (left) and Alan Merrick look on.

Tony Brown

Name: Tony Brown

Born: Oldham, 1945

Signed: 1961, as a trainee

Albion playing career: 1963–81

Clubs: Albion, New England Tea Men, Jacksonville Tea Men, Torquay United, Stafford Rangers

Albion appearances: 720

Albion goals: 279

England appearances: 1

Football League XI appearances: 2

Honours: League Cup winner 1965–66, FA Cup winner 1967–68, League Cup finalist 1967 and 1970

'Bomber' – Ultimate Record-Breaker

–LEGENDS–

Tony Brown

'They should erect a statue to Tony Brown in West Bromwich.' So said Ron Atkinson a decade and a half or so ago. Well now they are, and no Albion supporter is in the remotest doubt why.

For almost two decades, the man known as 'Bomber' blitzed opposition defences, increasingly so from a deep-lying position that made his well-timed runs into the danger area so difficult to check.

As befitting a man who has scored more goals for the club and made more appearances than any other man dead or alive, his feats are legendary … a goal in the FA Cup at Sheffield Wednesday that Bobby Charlton describes as the best he has ever seen, a stunning volley against Valencia, his precious promotion clincher at Oldham and seven goals in eight days against Nottingham opposition.

The choices of highlights are endless given that Brown scored the small matter of 279 times for the club, including one on his debut at Ipswich as a 17-year-old in 1963.

Having surpassed W G Richardson's figure, Brown went on, in 1978, to break Ronnie Allen's club record of 208 league goals – more than 50 ferociously struck penalties helping him on his way.

It was harsh on Brown that he only won a solitary England cap, although he had some consolation through representation for the youth team and Football League XI as well. He was also Midlands Footballer of the Year three times from 1969 to 1979, and finished First Division top marksman in 1970–71 with 28 goals.

All this from his 720 competitive Albion games – or 819 if we include friendlies. So that's why they are erecting that monument!

BELOW: 'Bomber' closes in on goal against Bolton in 1978.

131

A Vintage Era
1976-1982

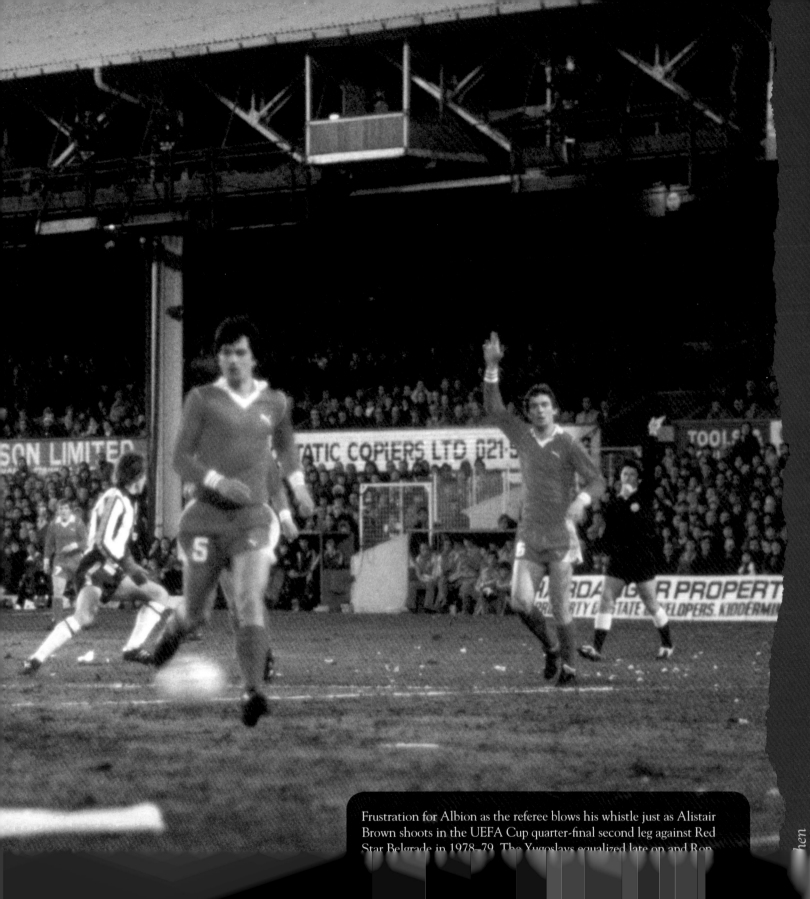

Frustration for Albion as the referee blows his whistle just as Alistair Brown shoots in the UEFA Cup quarter-final second leg against Red Star Belgrade in 1978–79. The Yugoslavs equalized late on and Red

1976 Johnny Giles, appointed the previous summer as Albion's first player-manager, leads the club to promotion in his first season; Giles then resigns but is persuaded to remain in charge for another year; a 4-0 home win against Manchester United underlines the Baggies' smooth return to top flight. **1977** Albion briefly threaten to qualify for Europe before finishing seventh – just above Arsenal, Everton and Leeds; Giles completes the signing of Laurie Cunningham from Leyton Orient while Ronnie Allen spots Cyrille Regis at Hayes and ensures he's Hawthorns-bound as well; Allen is appointed as Giles' successor but leaves after only six months. **1978** Ron Atkinson is installed following Allen's defection to Saudi Arabia; Big Ron's side embark on a thrilling FA Cup journey which ends in semi-final heartbreak; the club then go on an end-of-season tour of China; the final match of the year brings one of Albion's most famous results of the last 50 years – a 5-3 win at Manchester United. **1979** Albion lead the First Division in January and are considered genuine title challengers; David Mills arrives at The Hawthorns as British football's costliest signing; another near miss, a UEFA Cup quarter-final exit, is followed by a final third place in the league. **1980** Albion rebuild their main stand, the Halfords Lane side. **1981** Albion finish fourth in the First Division to make another (brief) entry into Europe; Atkinson's departure to Old Trafford is followed soon after by that of midfield stars Bryan Robson and Remi Moses; Ronnie Allen is reappointed. **1982** Albion reach the semi-finals of both domestic cups but also nearly go down.

RIGHT: Johnny Giles ... genial in his role as Albion's first player-boss.

Albion must have thought it could get no worse after they
lost 3-0 at Southampton on the opening day of 1975–76.
But when they returned to the Dell for an FA Cup fifth-
round replay six months later (right), they crashed 4-0, Len
Cantello and John Osborne being beaten here by Mike
Channon's shot. No problem … Johnny Giles' side were
outstanding for the most part of his first campaign at the
club and made rapid strides towards a First Division return.

BELOW: Accusing looks from (left to right) Ally Brown,
John Wile, Alistair Robertson and Paddy Mulligan in the
direction of Charlton striker Derek Hales during a game
in April 1976. The reason for their disapproval? John
Osborne lying prone and receiving treatment from physio
George Wright, following a challenge. Albion lost 2-1 at
the Valley but won three and drew one of their remaining
four games to secure promotion.

Sign Him Up!
Small Paws – and Then a BIG Finish!

One of the Hawthorns' more bizarre incidents is played out as David Cross rounds keeper Dai Davies to net one of the three first-half goals by which Albion easily beat Everton in November 1976. Claiming a major 'assist' was the club's new signing, Jack Russell, a four-legged intruder who so closed down the visitors' defenders when they were in possession that they gifted the ball to the grateful striker. There were baffled (and red) faces among the yellow shirts but the goal stood.

ABOVE: Albion were finding top-flight life very much to their liking by the time they recorded this 2-1 victory at Bristol City in April 1977. It was a seventh win in nine games – and a convincing follow-up to a nightmare 6-1 crash at Sunderland. Tony Godden is the keeper under pressure, having recently been called up to replace the veteran John Osborne.

RIGHT: Blonds have more fun … Derek Statham and Len Cantello deliberate over a free-kick at the start of an era in which Albion's football was exhilarating to watch.

A Laurie Load of Talent

The Hawthorns landscape changed dramatically when Johnny Giles signed Laurie Cunningham from Leyton Orient for only £100,000 in March 1977. The life of a black footballer in Britain was still troubled then but the Londoner immediately made himself a hit with Albion fans after making his debut close to his roots in a 2-0 victory at Tottenham. He then scored against Newcastle in his first home game and netted a further five times before the season was out. When Cyrille Regis came along a few months later, the mix was quite intoxicating...

ABOVE: The Three Degrees meet Albion's very own 'Three Degrees' – Laurie Cunningham (left), Brendon Batson (centre) and Cyrille Regis.

BELOW: Cunningham and Regis join The Hawthorns snow-shifters.

RIGHT: The joy of a Cunningham goal against Liverpool in 1978, celebrated with Len Cantello.

Goals,
Goals,
Goals!

LEFT: Unbridled delight on the Birmingham Road End as Ronnie Allen's Albion celebrate a goal in a 2-1 home win over Birmingham in the autumn of 1977. Cyrille Regis is the scorer of this one and (from left) Bryan Robson, Derek Statham, Len Cantello and Tony Brown are the men rushing in to add their congratulations. The above photo shows Laurie Cunningham being toasted by John Wile, Ally Robertson and Tony Brown in a 3-3 draw at West Ham. Albion came flying out of the blocks, with the Regis–Cunningham partnership central to their attacking potency.

Another Dash of Colour

Just as Albion fans must have wondered whether their lot could become any better, along came Ron Atkinson. Their side were flying high on an FA Cup run when The Hawthorns board turned to Cambridge United in January 1978, in the search for a successor to Ronnie Allen. Lift-off didn't come immediately, although a thrilling cup replay win over Manchester United later that month certainly helped. With Brendon Batson following the manager from Cambridge in the February, Albion overpowered Derby and Nottingham Forest to reach the semi-finals while also homing in on a top-six place in the table. The good times – *very* good – were coming.

A Bitter Disappointment at Highbury

Albion were seen as favourites to overcome Ipswich when, in 1978, they appeared in a record 18th FA Cup semi-final. But they played poorly and conceded two goals in the first 19 minutes, the first of them to their future player-manager Brian Talbot. That moment was doubly costly for Albion. Skipper John Wile suffered a badly gashed head in the process and eventually had to go off – hence his appearance in 'civvies' when the disappointed players acknowledged their fans on Highbury's North Bank at the end. Tony Brown (nearest camera) scored Albion's goal in a 3-1 defeat, Ipswich going on to lift the cup at Arsenal's expense. Thankfully, the side recovered from the heartache to qualify for Europe by finishing sixth in the league.

The iconic image of John Wile refusing to bow in the face of adversity in the 1978 FA Cup semi-final.

–LEGENDS–

John Wile

When we talk about courageous leaders, performing by sheer cussed example over and above the call of duty, we are speaking of men like John Wile.

For 12 and a half years, the gritty northeasterner was the kingpin of Albion's defence – a magnet when the ball was in the air and a craggy, composed figure when opponents tried to get the better of him on the ground.

It is a crying shame that Wile, like several other worthy team-mates, never won a major honour. A bit more so in his case as he played a colossal 619 competitive games while at The Hawthorns, to stand third behind Tony Brown and Alistair Robertson in the club's all-time appearances list.

The closest Wile came to silverware was three losing semi-finals – two of them in the FA Cup and the first marked by his reappearance in a bloodstained headband. He also skippered the Baggies to promotion in 1975–76 on what was almost a part-time arrangement by his standards. By playing 43 of the 48 matches, he was relatively 'in and out!' Remarkably, he was ever present in a club-record seven seasons, and totalled a mammoth 59 first-team league and cup matches in 1978–79 alone.

Wile, a true sportsman and ambassador, succeeded John Talbut at no 5, and could hardly have chosen a more fitting occasion on which to bow out. When he played at Sunderland in May 1983, he was not only making his 500th and last league appearance for the club but doing so at the club he had briefly served as a youngster before joining Peterborough.

In much later years, Wile was a member of Albion's board and served as their managing director.

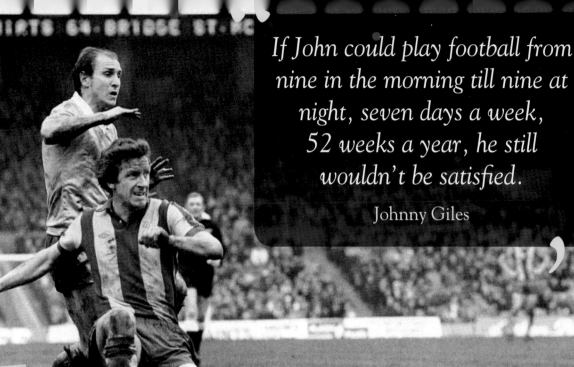

If John could play football from nine in the morning till nine at night, seven days a week, 52 weeks a year, he still wouldn't be satisfied.

Johnny Giles

FOOTBALL -STATS-

John Wile

Name: John Wile

Born: Sherborn, County Durham, 1947

Signed: 1970, from Peterborough

Albion playing career: 1970–83

Clubs: Sunderland, Peterborough, Albion, Peterborough

Albion appearances: 619

Albion goals: 29

England appearances: 0

Football League XI appearances: 0

Honours: Promotion winner 1975–76

ABOVE: In command while sliding the ball back to Tony Godden at Maine Road in 1981 – much to the frustration of Dennis Tueart.

RIGHT: Wile organizing the troops in a home derby against Aston Villa in 1978, where he had John Deehan (later an Albion team-mate) as an opponent.

147

Taking Europe by Storm

Albion were a breath of fresh air when they breezed into the 1978–79 UEFA Cup. Without a thought of bottling things up on their travels, they defeated Galatasaray 3-1 at home and away in the second round (left), then recorded another two-goal win when their journey took them to Portugal to take on Braga, who they then eliminated via an odd-goal success at The Hawthorns. It was when the draw for round four pitted them against Valencia, though, that the campaign really felt like it had come alive. Atkinson's men were outstanding on their trip to Spain's orange groves, emerging with a 1-1 draw (Ally Brown is pictured, below left, on a driving run at the Luis Casanova Stadium) that really should have been a victory. And no one did his reputation more good that night than goalscorer Laurie Cunningham, whose brilliant performance caught the eye of Real Madrid – the club he joined the following summer. Two goals by Tony Brown back in the Black Country did for Valencia – Argentine World Cup star Mario Kempes, West German ace Rainer Bonhof and all – but Albion unluckily fell to a deflected late goal at the next stage, when they went out 2-1 on aggregate to Red Star Belgrade.

Golden images from Albion's best ever night in Europe as (above) Tony Brown opens the scoring with an early penalty against Valencia in November 1978. 'Bomber' also rounded off the 2-0 home win with a superb volley just after half-time, the left photo showing the truncated celebrations after a Derek Statham goal that was disallowed for offside.

BELOW: The entrance of the teams in Belgrade. The gate of 90,000 was the biggest Albion have ever played in front of away from Wembley.

149

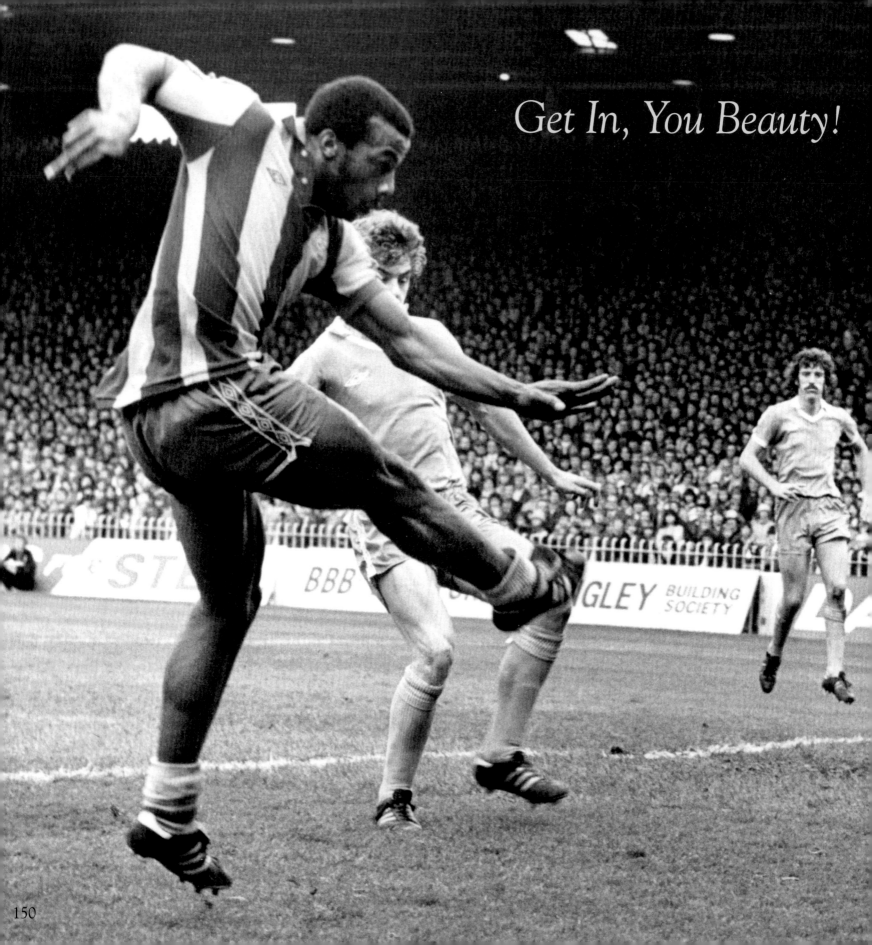

Get In, You Beauty!

Cyrille Regis thunders a near-post shot past Joe Corrigan (an Albion goalkeeper coach in recent years) in the 2-2 league draw at Manchester City in October 1978. Ron Atkinson's side had totalled 10 goals in their previous two games, including seven at home to Coventry.

LEFT: The subdued Willie Johnston, as captured before a penalty shoot-out in a pre-season tournament at Ibrox in August 1978.

BELOW: The more familiar version – during a game in September 1979.

BELOW LEFT: It may look like Johnston has just missed but he's actually expressing thanks after scoring in a League Cup tie at home to Exeter, whose defenders seem perplexed by his reaction.

ALBION SKATERS WALTZ TO TOP!

Jock's new boys spark a lift-off

We soon knew Bryan Robson (seen above on the rampage) was going to be a star. He scored two goals in his first three West Bromwich Albion games, and then overcame the huge setback of breaking his leg no fewer than three times. As a midfielder, a central defender or even a left-back, Robson oozed big-time potential and went on to net 46 times in 259 games for the club before being sold to Manchester United as Britain's costliest footballer. The pictures above left and below show Robson terrorizing Middlesbrough's defence and Albion looked every inch championship challengers as they followed up their famous 5-3 win at Manchester United by playing brilliantly on a white carpet to beat Bristol City on New Year's Day (above right). Later in 1978–79, though, the severe winter weather caused a spate of postponements and the side suffered a crucial loss of momentum that meant they sacrificed ground to Liverpool.

A Costly Failure in the Market

David Mills congratulates Bryan Robson on a goal at The Hawthorns – sadly, the gesture wasn't often returned. Mills became the most expensive player in British football when Ron Atkinson wrote Middlesbrough a cheque for £516,000 in January 1979. At the time, Albion were challenging hard for the title and Mills was seen as a prolific inside-forward. Sadly, circumstances soon changed – on both fronts. Mills bombed in the Black Country, managing only six goals in 76 games that were strung out over four years.

1979 – Goodbye To All This!

The style Albion fans missed and lamented when Laurie Cunningham was sold to Real Madrid for £995,000 in the summer of 1979. The left photo shows the genial Londoner preparing for his England under-21 debut against Scotland at Sheffield United in 1977. He scored the only goal of the game.

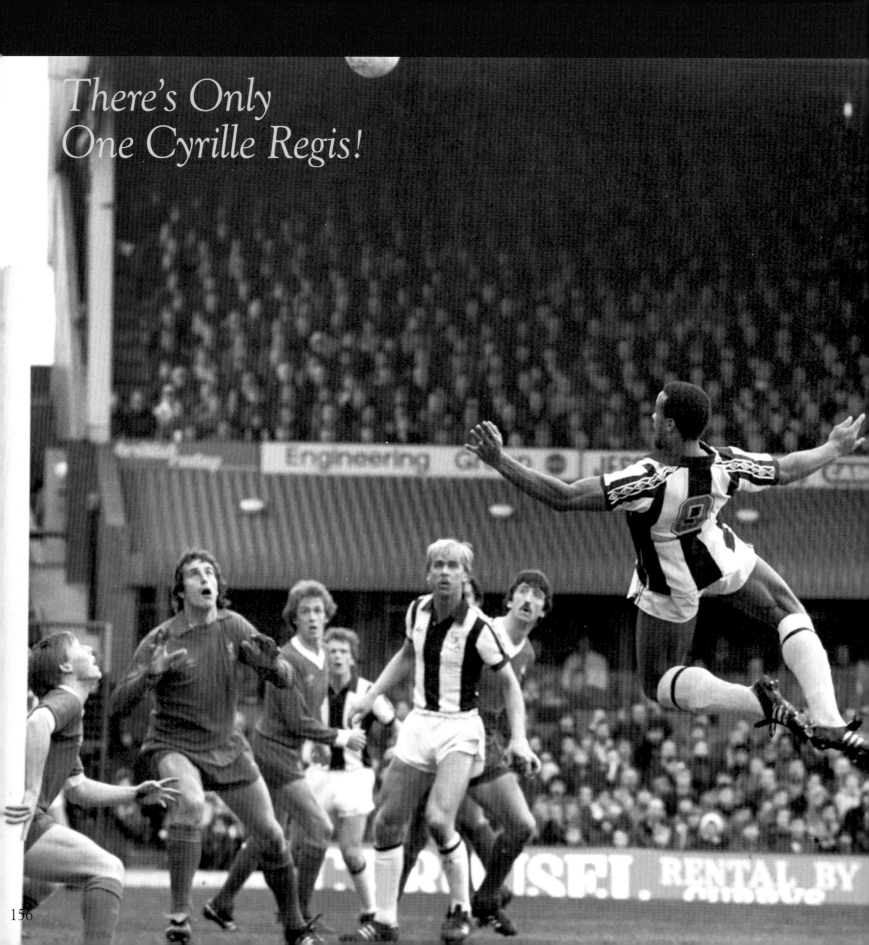

*There's Only
One Cyrille Regis!*

–LEGENDS–

Cyrille Regis

Cyrille Regis didn't just appear on The Hawthorns landscape in the second half of the 1970s. As near as a footballer can, he exploded into first-team stardom.

So stunning was his impact that the Birmingham Road End faithful knew immediately they had a new hero to laud.

Regis was all about raw power, muscle and dynamic finishing – knitted together, of course, by skills that made him look the real deal for several seasons.

The Londoner, snatched from Hayes for a pittance, didn't score many ordinary goals. The one against Middlesbrough on his league debut in September 1977 is still talked about at The Hawthorns; so, too, a solo effort at Manchester City in the same season. In-between came his two-goal contribution to an epic FA Cup replay win over Manchester United.

All told, Regis scored 18 times in that debut season, including twice in a League Cup home win over Rotherham on the night he was first introduced to senior football. He was 'box office', a devastating final link in the side fashioned by Johnny Giles, taken on by Ronnie Allen (the man who discovered him) and rounded off by Ron Atkinson.

Regis' early deeds were accomplished in partnership with Laurie Cunningham, with Brendon Batson then being recruited to complete what became known at the time as the 'Three Degrees'.

Briefly, Regis was becalmed, then he gained a second wind that saw him hit 17 goals in 1980–81 and 25 the following season, including absolute belters in the FA Cup against Norwich and Coventry.

He scored 112 times in 302 games for the club all told and might have won more than his five England caps. This guy was dynamite!

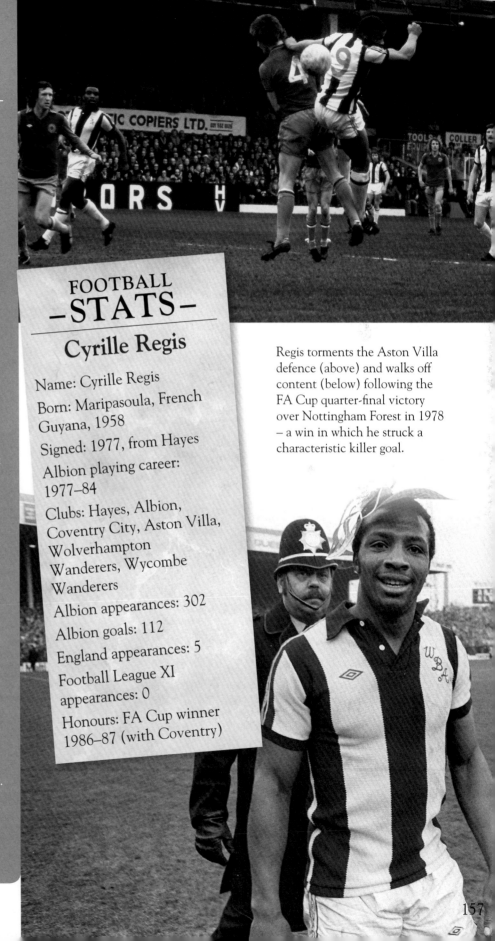

FOOTBALL –STATS–

Cyrille Regis

Name: Cyrille Regis

Born: Maripasoula, French Guyana, 1958

Signed: 1977, from Hayes

Albion playing career: 1977–84

Clubs: Hayes, Albion, Coventry City, Aston Villa, Wolverhampton Wanderers, Wycombe Wanderers

Albion appearances: 302

Albion goals: 112

England appearances: 5

Football League XI appearances: 0

Honours: FA Cup winner 1986–87 (with Coventry)

Regis torments the Aston Villa defence (above) and walks off content (below) following the FA Cup quarter-final victory over Nottingham Forest in 1978 – a win in which he struck a characteristic killer goal.

Football in the 1970s – in Black and White

In the wake of Laurie Cunningham's departure, Remi Moses made his league debut for Albion half-way through 1979-80 and was part of the line-up when a Cyrille Regis XI made up entirely of black players was selected to face an Albion team in Len Cantello's testimonial game. The midfielder is one in from the right on the front row while Brendon Batson and Stewart Phillips (the latter was a striker who was later to move to The Hawthorns) are either side of QPR keeper Derek Richardson and former Hawthorns youngster Ian Benjamin is on the far left of the back row. On the far right of those standing, next to the Wolves duo of George Berry and Bob Hazell, is Garth Crooks, who also had a spell with the Baggies in the 1980s. Far left at the front is Winston White – a Bobby Gould signing in the early 1990s. Two along from him is Cunningham, who moved to Real Madrid soon afterwards.

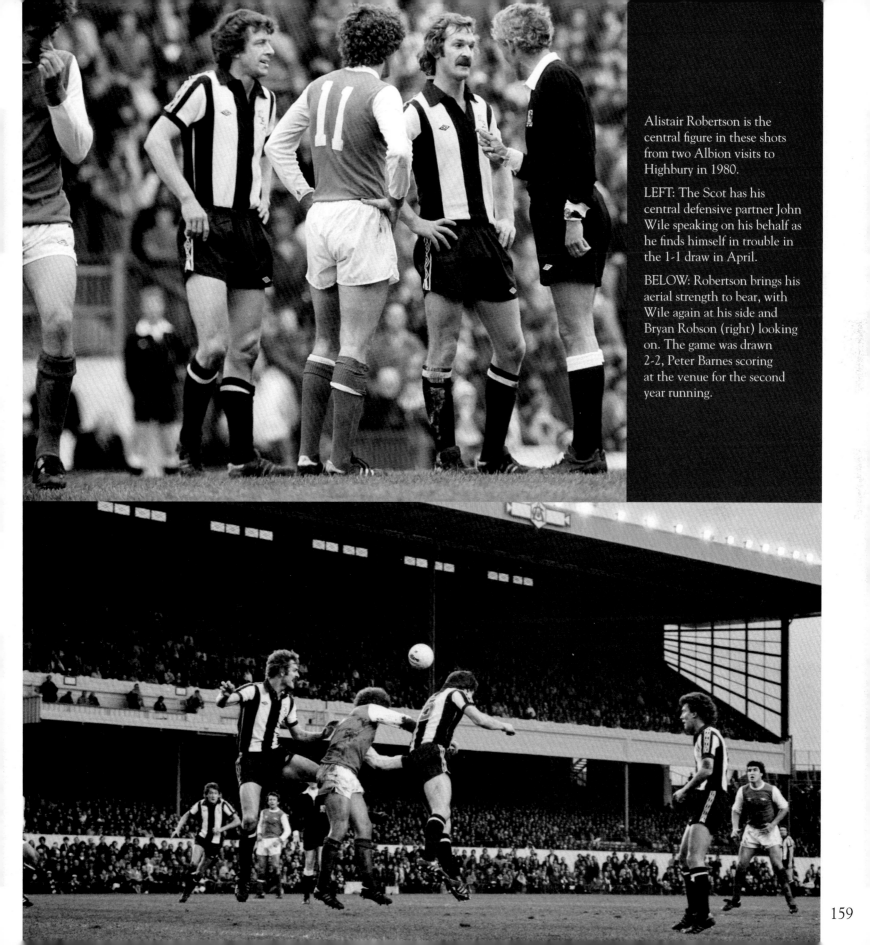

Alistair Robertson is the central figure in these shots from two Albion visits to Highbury in 1980.

LEFT: The Scot has his central defensive partner John Wile speaking on his behalf as he finds himself in trouble in the 1-1 draw in April.

BELOW: Robertson brings his aerial strength to bear, with Wile again at his side and Bryan Robson (right) looking on. The game was drawn 2-2, Peter Barnes scoring at the venue for the second year running.

Who's That On Our Touchline?

Brian Clough peers out from the dugout during a visit by his Nottingham Forest side to The Hawthorns. Nearest him, in view, is Albion's physio George Wright, while the club's long-serving former kit man, Dave Matthews, is closest to the camera.

Cloughie was a stated admirer of the Atkinson style and had good reason to be. The Albion manager got the better of the East Midlands legend in the 1978 FA Cup quarter-final, and oversaw home and away league draws against his side before the heartbreak of the final match of 1978–79, when Forest visited The Hawthorns and stole a late winner that left them runners-up to Liverpool, and their hosts in a final third place.

Despair in Liverpool's area as the seated Bryan Robson is congratulated by Remi Moses, John Deehan and second goalscorer Cyrille Regis after opening the scoring in Albion's 2-0 victory over the reigning league champions in February 1981.

It's Albion's turn for soul-searching ... Ally Robertson is the dejected man as Joe Jordan celebrates a Manchester United goal in a 2-1 home win at Old Trafford two months later.

ABOVE: Albion turn to the heavy artillery in their unsuccessful search for salvation at Maine Road in March 1981. John Wile, Alistair Brown, Martyn Bennett and John Deeham all lend their weight to this attack but Manchester City held on to win 2-1.

RIGHT: Crane operator Ray Flipper was certainly going up in the world when engaged to work on Albion's new £2m Halfords Lane Stand in the summer of 1981. Ron Atkinson's side had a head for heights, too, having finished fourth in the top flight the previous season and qualified again for Europe.

A familiar Hawthorns sight … Bryan Robson pausing for breath after running himself into the ground in Albion's cause.

For So Long a Baggie …

And Then a Red …

On 26th September 1981 Bryan Robson was still chasing lost causes for Albion – like this one, when he was up against Everton keeper Jim Arnold at Goodison Park. This was the last of his 198 league games for the club: only a midweek UEFA Cup appearance for them at home to Grasshoppers of Zurich remained. On 3rd October, Robson signed for Manchester United on the Old Trafford pitch just before kick-off against Wolves, becoming Britain's costliest footballer in the process. Robson was valued at £1.5m in a £2m deal that also took Remi Moses north. Damagingly for Albion, Ron Atkinson had made the same move that summer.

–LEGENDS–

Alistair Robertson

The Northeast was a fertile recruiting area for Albion in decades gone by. And Alistair Robertson's addition to a list that also included Bobby Hope, Doug Fraser and Asa Hartford proves Scotland was as well.

The craggy central defender arrived in 1968 and was still only 17 when he made his debut in front of 45,000 in a home victory over Manchester United in 1969.

Had it not been for a broken leg suffered against Charlton early in his career, Robertson would have played considerably more than the colossal number of league and cup games – 626, the second highest in Hawthorns history – with which he signed off in 1986.

There was also a substantial spell in the shadow of Dave Rushbury in 1974–75, but despite this Robertson was pretty much first choice for a decade and a half in which his commitment was total and his tackling fearsome. No wonder he also had a sizeable stint as captain.

Where Albion had been serial cup finalists in the 1960s and 1970, they repeatedly fell just short in the Robertson era, losing three semi-finals as well as a European quarter-final.

Robertson was ever present in the 1975–76 promotion campaign, though, and in 1979 passed Jimmy Dudley's club record of 166 consecutive First Division appearances.

What Scotland would now give for a defender of his stature! In a much more fruitful age north of the border, he didn't win a single international cap, although he played for his country's youths and schoolboys.

Finding one player like Robertson in a generation is something. The fact he played 573 games alongside John Wile underlines how blessed Albion were in this department of their side.

Robertson challenges Leeds' Terry Connor, supported by Derek Statham.

Still Going Strong!

BELOW: The 17-year-old Ally Robertson (far left) on his debut in October 1969 – a 2-1 home win over Manchester United.

FOOTBALL
–STATS–

Alistair Robertson

Name: Alistair Robertson

Born: Philpstoun, West Lothian, 1952

Signed: 1968, as a trainee

Albion playing career: 1968–86

Clubs: Albion, Wolverhampton Wanderers, Worcester City

Albion appearances: 626

Albion goals: 12

Scotland appearances: 0

Scottish League XI appearances: 0

Honours: Second Division promotion winner 1975–76, Fourth Division Championship winner 1987–88 (with Wolves), Sherpa Van Trophy winner 1987–88 (with Wolves), Third Division Championship winner 1988–89 (with Wolves)

And Still the Goals Came!

If opposition defences thought they were starting to get the better of Cyrille Regis (pictured here in the late 1970s), he was about to make them think again. With Ronnie Allen in charge for a second spell, the feared striker hit 25 goals in the 1981–82 season, with those against Norwich and Coventry in the FA Cup remembered as absolutely vintage efforts. Another pursuit of honours was on …

ABOVE: Ossie Ardiles, an early 1990s Hawthorns manager, unleashes a shot which is charged down by Derek Statham in the second leg of the League Cup semi-final at White Hart Lane in 1982. Albion had Martin Jol (a future Tottenham boss) sent off in the goalless first leg and were beaten by the only goal in the return.

LEFT: Happier scenes, reflected by Martyn Bennett's upstretched arm as Allen's men beat Coventry 2-0 at a sodden Hawthorns in the same season's FA Cup quarter-final.

Another Case of 'Almost' for the Nearly Men

Highbury heartache engulfed Albion once again in the spring of 1982 when they lost an FA Cup semi-final there for the second time in five seasons. This time it was Second Division QPR who inflicted the damage – thanks to a freak in-off from Clive Allen (seen here on the far right). Derek Statham and Martyn Bennett are the men attacking the ball. The season may have been worse for Albion. Despite their two outstanding cup runs, to which Cyrille Regis contributed a total of eight goals, they were nearly relegated. Only a last-week win over Leeds saved them – and sent the Yorkshiremen down instead.

Albion push for an equalizer in their 1-0 loss in the April during a nightmare run of seven consecutive league defeats.

Anfield, a fruitful hunting ground for Albion in the 1960s and early 1970s, had become much less inviting a decade or so on. Two trips in close proximity in 1982 brought defeats – their fifth and sixth in succession at the venue.

Peter Eastoe is beaten by Bruce Grobbelaar on the opening day of the 1982–83 season: a 2-0 beating that was quickly followed by two home victories, the second of them against Manchester United.

Goalkeeper Godden a Record-Breaker

By appearing in 228 consecutive first-team Albion games up to the autumn of 1981, Tony Godden has a club record in his hands. The keeper took over from John Osborne and, from the first day of the 1977–78 season, didn't miss a senior match for well over four years, in league or cups. By coincidence, his debut in March 1977 was at Tottenham – the ground at which he also finally lost his place to Mark Grew on the day Martin Jol was one of the scorers in a 2-1 Albion win. Jol is in the background here as Godden saves spectacularly in a 0-0 draw at Everton in November 1982, soon after one of his subsequent recalls.

Torrid Times
1983-1992

Tim Buzaglo is a name that still haunts West Bromwich Albion fans. He is pictured on his way to a hat-trick in January 1991, on the day non-league Woking won 4-2 at The Hawthorns in the FA Cup.

1983 Johnny Giles is reappointed as manager, taking over from Ron Wylie; the club's reserves win the Central League title for the first time since 1935; John Wile plays the last of his 619 league and cup matches for the Baggies. **1984** Cyrille Regis is sold to Coventry. **1985** Albion finish a healthy 12th in the top flight but attendances at the final three home games are 7,423 (the lowest at The Hawthorns for 28 years), 8,834 and (v Arsenal) 13,326; Giles resigns in the autumn of what becomes the club's worst ever season and his brother-in-law, Nobby Stiles MBE, takes over. **1986** Ron Saunders is appointed as manager in the February but is unable to prevent Albion finishing 18 points below the safety line; the former Aston Villa manager sells Steve Bull and Andy Thompson to Wolves for a combined £96,000, Alistair Robertson having already made the same move following 626 Baggies appearances. **1987** The club end the Second Division season with an average home crowd of 9,280 – the first time since 1910 the figure has dropped into four digits; Ron Atkinson takes over in the autumn for his second spell as manager; **1988** Albion avoid relegation by a point and Atkinson quits in the autumn to be replaced by player-boss Brian Talbot. **1991** Albion lose to Woking in the FA Cup and are relegated to the Third Division four months later for the first time. **1992** Bobby Gould, the manager who oversaw their drop, is sacked, having at least 'bequeathed' Bob Taylor to the club.

Alistair Robertson prepares to treat Terry Gibson to one of his trademark challenges in Albion's fourth-round 2-1 FA Cup away defeat to holders Tottenham in January 1983.

179

Hawthorns' gates reflected football's gloomy 1980s, and only 11,486 were present for this 1-1 draw against Stoke at a time when Albion were heading for another mid-table top-flight finish. The combined efforts on the line of Nicky Cross and Derek Statham failed to keep the ball out here, but Cross came up with the goal at the other end that staved off defeat. There was something to smile about with the breakthrough into the senior England side of Cyrille Regis, who won the first four of his five caps prior to his 1984 sale to Coventry.

Albion's board sent once more for Johnny Giles, with the side languishing in February 1984. The man who had brilliantly transformed the club's fortunes as a player-manager nearly a decade earlier had Nobby Stiles (left) and Norman Hunter at his side and, despite a first-game FA Cup defeat at home to Plymouth, the early signs were good. On successive Saturdays, their team won at Tottenham, beat Stoke 3-0 and recorded a 2-0 home win over Manchester United (below). Garry Thompson, Martyn Bennett, Derek Statham and Tony Grealish are the Baggies men anxiously watching this shot from Arthur Graham, while the visiting player hoving into view on the extreme right is none other than Bryan Robson.

How Did It Come To This?

Empty seats aplenty as Albion attack against Portsmouth. For more years in the 1980s and early 1990s than supporters care to remember, the club were deep in the doldrums. In 1986–87, the average league attendance at The Hawthorns fell below 10,000, and Second Division survival became the main priority. At least striker Don Goodman, pictured here leading the aerial onslaught, proved to be a ray of hope after arriving from Bradford in 1987.

Now Big Ron's Back!

Despite what proved to be the failure of appointing Johnny Giles for the second time – even the genial Irishman admitted: 'It was the wrong thing to do' – Albion made another delve into their past when they sought a successor to the unpopular Ron Saunders in 1987. They went for Ron Atkinson and his original Hawthorns assistant Colin Addison, and the duo were all smiles when paraded before the cameras early in the club's second season of Second Division football. Certainly, they looked happier than when Big Ron had been a loser while sitting in the visitors' dugout (above) with Manchester United earlier in the decade. On his right shoulder in that photo is Mick Brown, who had succeeded Addison when joining forces with him at The Hawthorns first time round then followed him to Old Trafford. Big Ron's second reign in the Black Country was not a success. Albion just stayed up in 1987–88 and were mid-table when he took off for Atlético Madrid the following October. Even before Giles and Atkinson, Albion had given Ronnie Allen two spells in charge.

Rowley Regis-born Carlton Palmer, having been blooded in Albion's first team in the nightmare 1985–86 season, soon became a regular and played 139 first-team games for the club in all. He won few points for artistic content, before or after his 1989 move to Sheffield Wednesday, but graduated to the full England team and even played in the 1992 European Championships finals in Sweden.

Big Day in Another Dismal Season

Decent runs in the two cups lifted what was another tough campaign for Albion fans in 1989–90. The club made it through two rounds of both competitions and reached this FA Cup fifth-round date with Aston Villa. They lost 2-0, though, and finished only two rungs above the relegation line.

Don Goodman, the striker who lit up Albion's 1989–90 campaign by becoming the first man in nearly 20 years to score over 20 league goals for the club in a season.

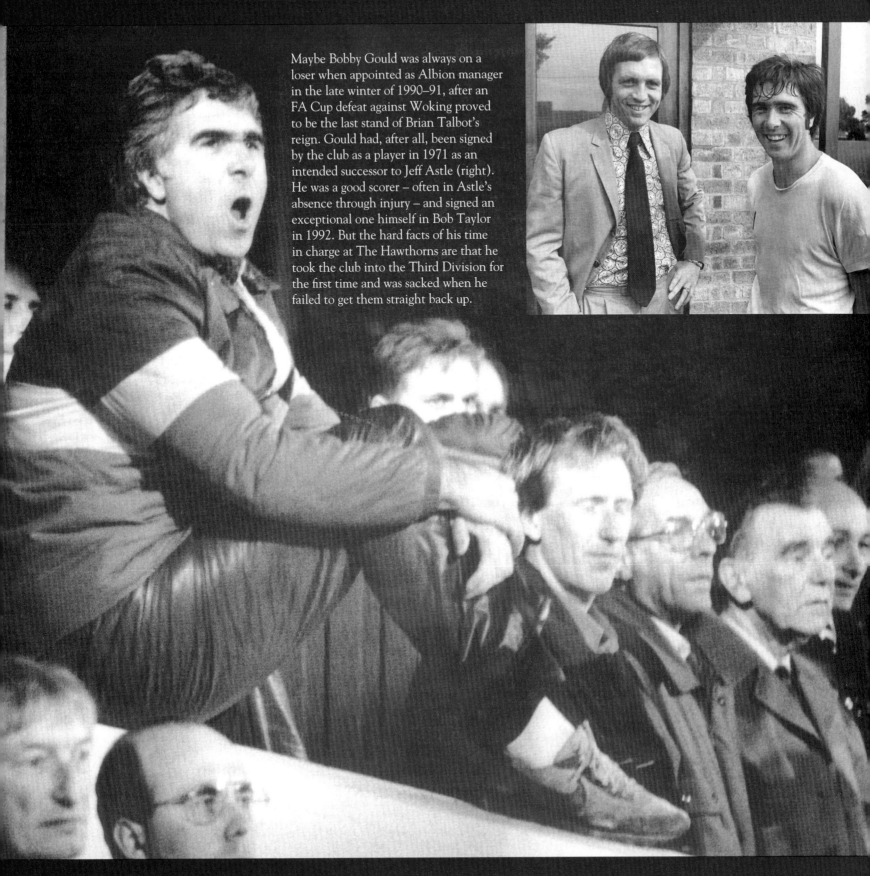

Maybe Bobby Gould was always on a loser when appointed as Albion manager in the late winter of 1990–91, after an FA Cup defeat against Woking proved to be the last stand of Brian Talbot's reign. Gould had, after all, been signed by the club as a player in 1971 as an intended successor to Jeff Astle (right). He was a good scorer – often in Astle's absence through injury – and signed an exceptional one himself in Bob Taylor in 1992. But the hard facts of his time in charge at The Hawthorns are that he took the club into the Third Division for the first time and was sacked when he failed to get them straight back up.

On the Way Back!
1993-2002

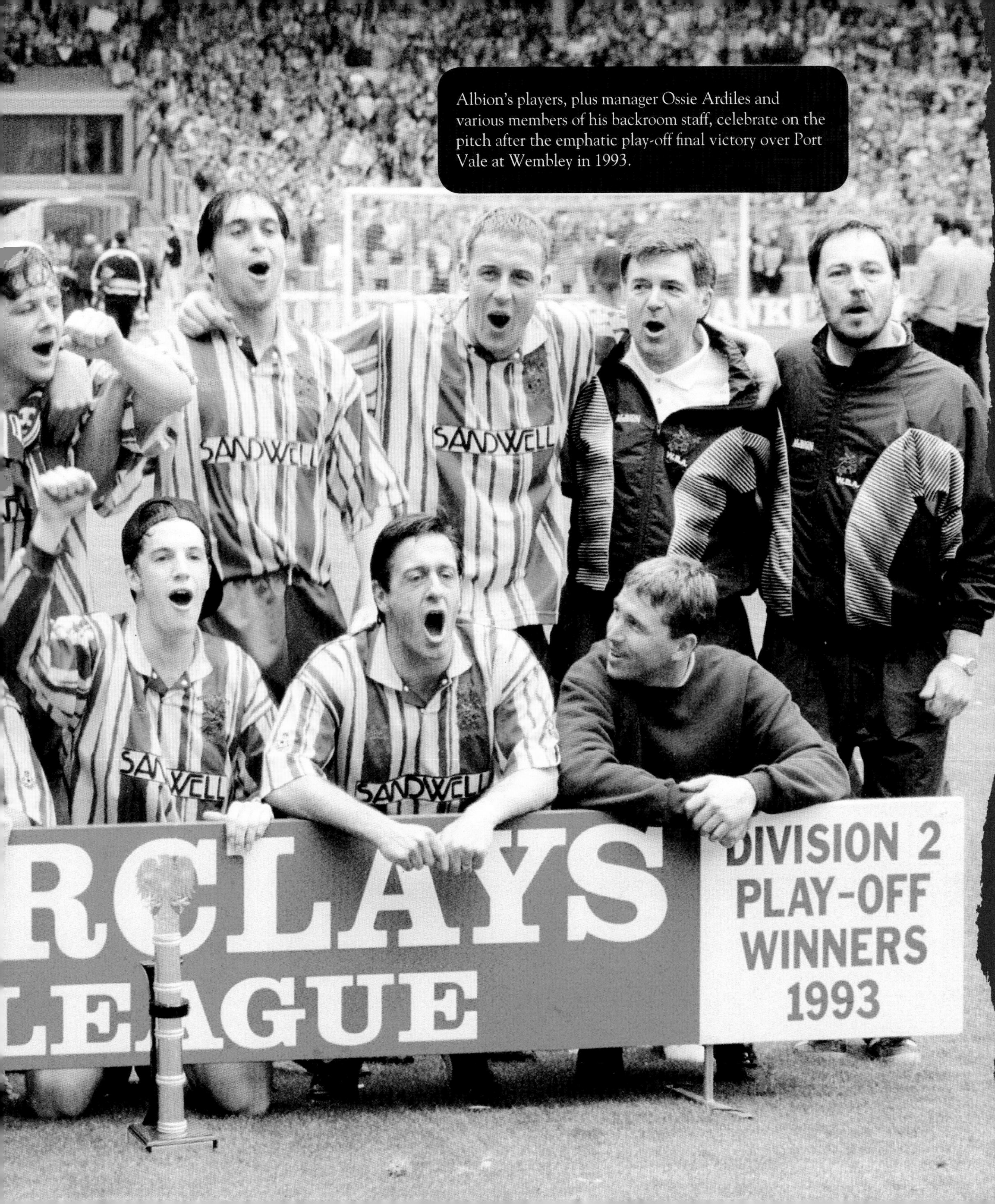

Albion's players, plus manager Ossie Ardiles and various members of his backroom staff, celebrate on the pitch after the emphatic play-off final victory over Port Vale at Wembley in 1993.

DIVISION 2
PLAY-OFF
WINNERS
1993

1993 Bob Taylor takes his goal tally for the season into the 30s – the first Albion player to do so since Tony Brown in 1970–71; Ossie Ardiles' 'boing boing' Baggies defeat Swansea in a two-leg play-off semi-final, then overpower Port Vale 3-0 in the final; Ossie Ardiles resigns in the summer and is replaced by his former Tottenham boss, Keith Burkinshaw. **1994** Albion ensure survival back in the second grade by winning at Portsmouth on the last day; Alan Buckley is appointed as manager; the redeveloped and redesigned Hawthorns is officially opened on Boxing Day. **1995** Albion embark on a nightmare run of 11 successive league defeats in a 14-game run in league and FA Cup matches containing 13 defeats and a draw. **1997** Ray Harford succeeds Buckley as boss and immediately appoints Cyrille Regis as a coach; Harford jumps ship in less than a year to join QPR and is replaced by Denis Smith – Albion's 12th manager in 15 years. **1998** Albion, stuck in the middle of the (new) First Division for several years, embark on their 100th season of league football. **1999** Brian Little has a brief spell in charge after succeeding Smith in the summer. **2000** Gary Megson arrives at the helm and sees his side win two of their final three matches, saving themselves from relegation at the expense of neighbours, Walsall; Jason Roberts becomes the club's first £2m player. **2001** Albion hold a 2-0 lead during the home first leg of the play-off semi-final but Bolton come back to win, and later prevail in the final. **2002:** Albion sensationally overhaul Wolves, finish as runners-up to Manchester City and reach the Premier League for the first time.

Andy Hunt leaps over the outstretched legs of Dean Glover as Albion, having hit back from a first-leg deficit to beat Swansea in the semi-finals, assert their supremacy over Port Vale in the final at Wembley. It was the club's first visit to the stadium in 23 long years and there had been some very fallow times in-between, especially in the second half of the 1980s and the early 1990s.

Ian Hamilton is congratulated by Gary Strodder after scoring what proved to be the winner against Swansea in the play-off semi-final. It was a night on which The Hawthorns went boing-boing crazy for the first time.

Precious memories from Albion's 3-0 Wembley victory over Port Vale … the Andy Hunt header which broke a tense 69-minute deadlock by giving Ossie Ardiles' men the lead – and the congratulations for fellow scorer Kevin Donovan from Ian Hamilton (centre) and Simon Garner. Full-back Nicky Reid struck Albion's second goal on an afternoon on which Bob Taylor was surprisingly absent from the score sheet. Vale's task was made all the harder by the sending-off of central defender Peter Swan with the scores still level.

Second Division play-off final 1993

Date & Venue: 30th May 1993 at Wembley

Result: West Bromwich Albion 3 Port Vale 0

West Bromwich Albion: Lange, Reid, Lilwall, Bradley, Raven, Strodder, Hunt (Garner, 89), Hamilton, Taylor, McNally, Donovan.
Substitute: Robson

Port Vale: Musselwhite, Aspin, Kent (Billing, 63), Porter, Swan, Glover, Slaven, Van Der Laan (Cross, 82), Foyle, Kerr, Taylor

Goals: Hunt (69 min), Reid (83 min), Donovan (89 min)

Attendance: 53,471

Captain: Darren Bradley

Manager: Ossie Ardiles

> *I've never seen support like that before. It was magnificent.*
>
> Keith Burkinshaw

LEFT: A section of the 42,000-strong Albion following at Wembley in 1993 – the largest the club have ever taken to a game away from The Hawthorns. It would have been bigger still but for segregation problems. Vale's fans were outnumbered well over three to one in a crowd of 53,471.

RIGHT: Nicky Reid, scorer of the second goal at Wembley, is supported by Bernard McNally as he cuts past Robin van der Laan. Reid was only a substitute in the semi-final when Albion overturned a 2-1 deficit against Swansea despite finishing the home second leg with only nine men, Micky Mellon and Colin West both being sent off.

–LEGENDS–

Bob Taylor

As one of only nine men to have scored over 100 league goals for West Bromwich Albion, Bob Taylor already has a cherished place in Hawthorns history.

Add to that the fact that one of those goals came on the tense afternoon on which the club guaranteed First Division survival in 2000, and another followed two years later when promotion to the Premier League was secured for the first time, and the idolatry becomes even more understandable.

Taylor's statistics stand the test of time in any era but the fact he delivered so handsomely at a time when Albion were on their knees makes his contribution all the more valuable.

He was signed halfway through the first of the club's two seasons in the third grade in the early 1990s, scoring once on his debut (against Brentford) and twice in his first away game (against Birmingham). But the eight goals in 19 league matches he managed in 1991–92 were dwarfed by what came next.

His tally in the promotion-winning 1992–93 campaign was an astonishing 37, and the 21 he managed the following season were the main reason the club just clung on to their regained status.

'Super Bob' departed for Bolton in 1998, then made a triumphant curtain call when ditching a club in the FA Cup semi-final for one embroiled in another relegation scrap. With five goals in the last six games, he was probably the difference …

Taylor, who had attracted bids from Coventry and Sheffield United in his prime, was awarded a testimonial in 2003 and the tributes poured in.

So Albion did have something to be grateful for from Bobby Gould's reign after all!

Super Bob!

FOOTBALL
–STATS–

Bob Taylor

Name: Bob Taylor

Born: Horden, County Durham, 1967

Signed: January 1992 from Bristol City

Albion playing career: 1992–98 and 2000–03

Clubs: Leeds United, Bristol City, Albion, Bolton Wanderers, Albion, Cheltenham Town, Tamworth

Albion appearances: 377

Albion goals: 131

England appearances: 0

Football League XI appearances: 0

Honours: Second Division promotion winner 1992–93, First Division promotion winner 1996–97 (with Bolton), First Division promotion winner 2001–02

Lee Ashcroft was Albion's man of the moment on the tense last day of the 1993–94 First Division season. Keith Burkinshaw's side needed three points to be sure of staying up – and achieved them thanks to the winger's goal in a 1-0 victory at Portsmouth. Bernard McNally is the team-mate up in support of Ashcroft here, with Paul Raven and Tony Lange in the background and, beyond them, a large section of the club's huge 10,000 following at Fratton Park.

The moment when Albion fans dared to believe their side were heading to the Premier League – a year before they actually made it. Lee Hughes beats Matt Clarke with a penalty and puts Gary Megson's men 2-0 up in the home first leg of their play-off semi-final against Bolton in 2001. But the visitors hit back to draw 2-2, win the return 3-0, and go on to emerge victorious against Preston in the final at the Millennium Stadium.

The Infamous Battle of Bramall Lane

If it's controversy and incident you like, Sheffield United 0 Albion 3 on 16th March 2002, was the match for you. Stunning goals, violent outpourings, sendings-off, injuries, even an abandonment … this was a game that had the lot, yet left no one celebrating.

First to see red was United keeper Simon Tracey for handling outside his area after nine minutes. Scott Dobie soon put Albion ahead with a superbly worked headed goal and Derek McInnes doubled the lead with a spectacular 20-yarder midway through the second half. Then the game exploded with the dismissals, in quick succession, of Georges Santos and fellow substitute Patrick Suffo – both within a few seconds of them going on. Former Baggies man Santos lunged in two-footed and dangerously on Andy Johnson, who had to be taken off, and Suffo headbutted skipper McInnes (right) yet was still so incensed that he had to be dragged off (below right) by coach Kevin Blackwell and Phil Jagielka.

Dobie added a third goal and briefly found time to rejoice with Neil Clement (facing page) but, with Michael Brown and Rob Ullathorne going off injured and the Blades down to six players, referee Eddie Wolstenholme ended the game eight minutes early.

Sheffield-born Gary Megson, who still lived in the city, was visibly upset afterwards (facing page) and promised that, if his side were made to replay the game, they would kick off and then walk off the field. The Football League subsequently ruled that the result should stand and the FA fined the home club £10,000. Santos and Suffo were immediately transfer-listed and never played for the Blades again.

Albion's 3-0 win reduced the gap between them and second-placed Wolves, and turned up the heat in an extraordinary Black Country head-to-head race for automatic promotion behind Kevin Keegan's Manchester City.

The unbelievable became reality in the spring of 2002 when Albion pegged back what seemed like an unassailable lead over them to claim the second automatic promotion place behind Manchester City. It all boiled down to the last afternoon, but Gary Megson's men kept their nerve to beat Crystal Palace 2-0 and finish three points ahead of their neighbours, their extraordinary eight-game run-in containing seven victories and a draw. Darren Moore got the party started by opening the scoring against Palace with this opening goal – and a celebration to match. Big Dave's fellow defender Russell Hoult wrote his own piece of history by keeping a club record of 27 clean sheets in a season.

A Sunday Afternoon Walk with the Family

Not once but twice, Gary Megson took Albion to the Premier League. Having inherited a relegation-threatened side and then been beaten 14 months later in the play-offs, he inspired the surge to runners-up spot in 2001–02 and repeated the feat in 2003–04. He is the only Albion manager ever to lead the club to the top flight twice.

Going Up, Going Crazy!

On wet and windy days, the author has no wish to relinquish his seat in the relative comfort of the press box. A look at all these magnificent pictures, though, reminds him of the quite brilliant work carried out by the photographers at pitch-side and he wishes to salute the many 'snappers' on the *Daily Mirror* – and associated titles such as the *Birmingham Post & Mail* – whose expertise has brought this publication to life.

He also wishes to thank all at Mirrorpix and Haynes Publishing for their help and guidance, in particular David Scripps, Vito Inglese, Mel Sambells, Elizabeth Stone, Richard Havers, Kevin Gardner and Rebecca Ellis, and give a special nod to his good pal Laurie Rampling for hours of invaluable guidance and the loan of a host of items for these pages. Also, to John Homer for all his knowledge and diligence on matters historical, and to Albert McPherson and his family.

Other picture credits:

Laurie Rampling: Top photo page 49, top right photo page 56, bottom right page photo page 59, bottom left photo page 63, bottom photo page 131, photo page 134, photo page 137, photo page 143, bottom photo page 147, top photo page 148, top photo page 157, top photo page 170.

Dean Walton and family: Top photo page 43.

Howard Talbot: page 57

Albert McPherson and family: photos on pages 76 and 77, and top photo page 78.

—